T0178994

Darknet

Computing and Connected Society Set

coordinated by
Dominique Carré and Geneviève Vidal

Volume 2

Darknet

Geopolitics and Uses

Laurent Gayard

 WILEY

First published 2018 in Great Britain and the United States by ISTE Ltd and John Wiley & Sons, Inc.

ISTE Ltd
27-37 St George's Road
London SW19 4EU
UK

www.iste.co.uk

John Wiley & Sons, Inc.
111 River Street
Hoboken, NJ 07030
USA

www.wiley.com

Library of Congress Control Number: 2018932685

British Library Cataloguing-in-Publication Data
A CIP record for this book is available from the British Library
ISBN 978-1-78630-202-1

Contents

Preface

"According to Stanford[1], by 2030, we will have 130 billion objects connected to the Internet. Even our hands and our hearts no doubt, everything will be connected. What is the governance framework? What public policy will regulate this?"[2] Fadi Chehadé, director of ICANN's 55th Congress, summed up some of the issues raised in this book, by asking these questions during the "high-level government meeting" of several government officials. The statement from the president of the powerful *Internet Corporation for Assigned Names and Numbers* recalls the importance of the ongoing global negotiations between governments, intergovernmental organizations and international institutions on the issue of Internet governance. Since its inception in 1998, ICANN has assumed the essential and strategic role of managing domain names and electronic addressing on the Internet and is a private law organization. However, it is subject to the courts and the U. S. Chamber of Commerce and is therefore dependent on the U.S. government. In 2014, the United States agreed to initiate a transition process paving the way for the internationalization of ICANN and thus, in part, Internet governance. Internationalization or privatization? The future of the Internet depends on resolving this issue,

---

1 Stanford University. Private American University, located in the heart of Silicon Valley, south of San Francisco. In 1968, Stanford University was linked to the University of Los Angeles (UCLA) and the University of Utah through the first offshore computer network that took the name ARPANET and foreshadowed the creation of the Internet.

2 Fadi Chehadé, Director of the *Internet Corporation for Assigned Names and Numbers* (ICANN). 55th ICANN Congress, Marrakech, March 7, 2016.

which remains a source of conflict in the current state of negotiations. These discussions between States, private stakeholders, user communities and international organizations, about the evolution of international jurisdiction that frames the development of the global network, reveal how Internet governance is a major geopolitical issue. While these negotiations were taking place at the highest level, the scale of cyber-attacks that hit hundreds of countries and institutions around the world in May and June 2017, and an even higher number in private institutions, suddenly brought a new type of conflict and criminal activity to the front lines, using cyberspace as its setting. Parallel to the debate on the future status of ICANN, the *Darknet* phenomenon, which encompasses all encrypted, private and alternative networks on the Internet, alternatively raises the issue of network governance and control through the prism of cybersecurity and the preservation of anonymity and freedom of Internet users, another debate, no less essential, which has become even more acute since Edward Snowden's revelations. Because darknets – it is more accurate to speak of "hidden networks" in the plural – participate in an anarchic development of the global network, which is largely beyond the control of states and ICANN, and also because the tools of future wars and computer attacks are exchanged at the heart of these new virtual territories, this book will be devoted to the history and geopolitics of the darknet. Therefore, it will be necessary to start by defining the terms used, starting with darknet and darknets, a plural term to designate various private or encrypted networks, such as Tor (*The Onion Router*), I2P or Freenet, and a singular term to encompass the whole phenomenon of the "hidden Internet". The shift from plural to singular in itself sums up some 15 years of evolution and the transition from the first peer-to-peer (P2P) to the genuine nebula of parallel networks, an evolution that will be discussed at length in this book. An attempt will therefore be made here to differentiate the different spaces that constitute the "network of networks" today ("surface web", "deep web" and "hidden networks"), to explain some essential notions such as network neutrality and to highlight the role of Internet governance operators, such as ICANN. We will then discuss the genealogy of the phenomenon of darknets, which has been placed in the history of the Internet and the transformations of cyberspace. We will try to analyze which cultures are linked to the constitution of the communities and spaces that make up these new virtual territories and lastly, the security, geopolitical and economic implications of this new (r)evolution of the digital universe that we have taken the liberty of calling "Internet 3.0"[3]. We hope that this book will at least partially enlighten the reader on the essential issues of the transformation of the communication society that could change digital usage, public policy and, of course, our daily life in the near future.

Laurent GAYARD

February 2018

_____

3 By clearly distinguishing this expression from "Web 3.0" that implies the "Internet of Things".

Introduction

On October 17, 2011, the Anonymous group launched a "darknet operation", revealing the existence of some forty pedophile sites hosted on the Tor network[1]. The accounts of 1,626 users of these sites were put online and the operation led to the closure of the targeted sites, but the authorities were concerned about the ability of groups such as Anonymous to seriously interfere with ongoing police operations in this type of case. The case also helped to accredit and popularize the idea that there would be a "deep Internet", providing safe haven for activities under the guise of a vast virtual lawless zone. A year and a half later in August 2013, the FBI's dismantling of a vast network of child pornography on the Tor network, followed by the arrest of Ross Ulbricht in October of the same year, accused of administering Silk Road, an online drug dealing site, helped fuel the dark legend. The darknet has therefore crossed the threshold of confidentiality and moved from a rumor to a social phenomenon, to the point of capturing French Interior Minister Bernard Cazeneuve's attention, who in March 2016, did not hesitate to assert in a political context, marked by a wave of murderous attacks and a state of emergency: "Those who hit us use the darknet and encrypted messaging", he said. A phenomenon known very little of until then, the existence of hidden networks such as Tor, the "onion router"[2], reached a little media fame at the time.

---

1 http://www.humanite.fr/medias/un-reseau-de-plus-de-1500-%C2%AB-pedophiles-%C2%BB-demantele-par-anonymous-482267.

2 Attributing to sites and users connected to the Tor network addresses in ".onion" instead of the classic ".com" or ".fr".

In 2016, Sir David Omand, former director of GCHQ[3], noted in the pages of the *World Policy Journal* [OMA 16] that: "The so-called darknet is where most of the online criminal activity takes place, largely beyond the reach of law enforcement. On the darknet, anonymity is the rule, and the identity and location of the participants can be concealed from even the most persistent gaze of police and intelligence agencies". While using the singular term, David Omand nevertheless took care to restore the term darknet to its multiple singularity, which refers to a disparate aggregate of virtual places, since there are actually as many darknets as there are encrypted and private networks. "The darknet is a collection of networks and technologies used to share digital content", explained Peter Biddle, Paul England, Marcus Peinado and Bryan Willman in 2003, typically considered to be the first individuals to use the term in an article published in 2003. The darknet is not a physically separate network, but applications and a layer of protocols superimposed on existing networks. The four authors included P2P networks, key-protected exchange systems and even electronic messaging, private forums and newsgroups[4] in the denomination of darknets, the term already pluralized. As early as 2003, the four researchers predicted the irremediable expansion of this phenomenon [BID 03]: "We expect that the effectiveness of the darknet as a distribution mechanism will run into some obstacles in the short term, but ultimately, the genius of the darknet will be indelible".

In 2003, Biddle, England, Peinado and Willman combined the idea of the darknet exclusively with illegal distribution networks for licensed content. The problem that arose at that time, synthesized in the study of the four engineers, was still limited to illegal downloading and the threat posed by this growing phenomenon to the cultural industry. But if the origin of the darknet concept can be linked to the development of illegal download networks, the term also refers to a specific culture linked to technological developments marking the turn of the 20th and 21st century. On February 8, 1996, U.S. President Bill Clinton signed the Telecommunications Act, accompanied by the Communications Decency Act. This initiative

---

3 *Government Communications Headquarters* (GCHQ).

4 *The Network News Transfer Protocol* (NNTP) is a network protocol designated by URLs beginning with news: //. For example, the Usenet network system, invented in 1979, is organized around the principle of newsgroups, which are hierarchical according to different themes, to which a user can subscribe according to their preferences. Newsgroups allow the exchange of articles and even image, audio or video files in some cases.

represented a historic step in the process of liberalizing telecommunications and online services such as the Internet. The Telecommunications Act replaced the old Communications Act of 1934, attempting to take into account the radical changes in American society during the 1960s, 1970s and 1980s. The main idea of the legislation was to foster the development of competition in the telecommunications sector and to facilitate the entry of large private groups into a sector originally dominated by the American Telephone & Telegraph Corporation. Initially intended to promote the opening up of the telecommunications market to multiple groups, the Telecommunications Act actually led to the creation of new telecommunication giants and the disappearance of a large number of minor operators in this sector. Many observers accused the Telecommunications Act of having paved the way for the complete domination of the mass media. In this case, the new legislation allowed a few major operators to take over the market of internet access providers, such as UUNet (now Verizon), Sprint Corporation, Level 3 Communication (acquired on October 31, 2016 by Centurylink), Comcast and AT&T. In the aftermath of Bill Clinton's announcement that he had signed the Telecommunications Act, John Perry Barlow, co-founder of the Electronic Frontier Foundation[5], drafted a "Declaration of Independence of Cyberspace"[6], in which he stated that no government, corporation or institution should impose its authority or claim on any property rights over the Internet. In particular, the declaration, which was addressed to governments and leaders of major economic consortia, proclaimed: "You are not welcome here. You have no sovereignty where we meet. We form our own social contract". The "cyber-revolutionary" rhetoric, such as that of John Perry Barlow, may seem quite fanciful today. However, it still applies today, through multiple small groups, individual operators, sites and discussion forums, fervently defending the idea of a "Freenet" instead of a darknet, in order to reintroduce the name given to the social network created in 2010: an anonymous and free Internet 3.0, on which the user always remains "in control".

However, 20 years after the publication of the "Declaration of Independence of Cyberspace", times have changed, as has the Internet.

---

5 Founded in 1990 in the United States by Mitch Kapor, John Gilmore and John Perry Barlow, the Electronic Frontier Foundation's main objective is to defend freedom of expression on the Internet.
6 See the text in Appendix 1.

According to figures from the Data Observatory[7], the global volume of online databases has reached 4.4 zettabytes[8]. The International Data Center[9] predicts that this global volume will increase 10-fold by 2020 to 44 zettabytes[10]. The exponential rate of development of the Internet today makes any calculation partially obsolete: some authors state a trillion pages have been created, that is to say a thousand billion, etc. [PIS 08, p. 188]. This exponential growth interests public and private companies, anxious to take advantage of the economic opportunities offered by the "deep web" and "Big Data". It also opens up new opportunities for all those who intend to benefit from the growth of the global network, which increasingly calls into question the ability of state structures to effectively monitor the multiple networks that make up the Internet today. This desire to escape the control of institutions responds to economic and ideological motivations and is in line with the promises, sometimes illusory, of a globalized system that makes all forms of borders, barriers and regulations obsolete.

The recent development of darknets, which are no longer just networks of exchange, but real layers of alternative networks superimposed on the global network, contains all the questions raised by the exponential growth of intangible flows, the modification of digital usage and the questioning of the regulatory status of States. The latter, as well as the security and intelligence agencies that depend on them, are now becoming aware of the danger attached to the idea of virtual lawless zones that are somewhat or totally beyond their control. All of them are therefore stepping up their efforts to develop credible and effective policies in the field of cybersecurity. The resurgence of terrorism, but also other illegal activities such as trafficking in

---

7 Data Observatory, July 2014, IDC study for EMC-Digital Universe.

8 1 zettabyte = 1,000 exabytes, that is to say 1,021 bytes, the basic unit measuring the volumes of digital information. By way of comparison, 1 zettabyte corresponds to 152 million years of viewing standard VHS cassettes.

9 In 1976, a group of scientists founded the GSE (Group of Scientific Experts) in Geneva at the end of the Geneva Conference on Disarmament in order to study technological developments. Between 1984 and 1995, a series of experiments on improving data collection were carried out jointly by American, Russian and Swedish scientists. In 1996, after the creation of the Comprehensive Nuclear-Test-Ban Organization (CBTO), the International Data Center was transferred from Arlington, Virginia, to Vienna, Austria, to officially become the IDC. Since then, this international organization has generated independent studies and data analysis in a wide range of fields.

10 According to linguist Mark Liberman, this is the equivalent of all the words and languages spoken on the planet.

drugs, weapons and human beings, which are using new technologies in order to develop, is giving rise to policies for the security and surveillance of cyberspace. In turn, they are severely criticized and questioned by some sections of civil society who, on the contrary, highlight the usefulness of these spaces where anonymity is relatively preserved for journalists or dissidents threatened by authoritarian regimes, thus allowing the free flow of information and freedom of expression. However, States are also using the capabilities offered by darknets to create a new form of interstate or asymmetrical conflict for themselves, that is now taking place in virtual space, but has very severe consequences in the form of cyber-attacks, such as the large-scale one that took place in Estonia in 2007, inaugurating the entry into a new dimension of modern warfare. While, according to journalist Duncan Campbell [CAM 07], States have been losing the battle of cryptography to prevent the spread of advanced encryption techniques in civil society since the 1990s, it seems that Tor-like encrypted networks now offer capabilities to resist cyber-attacks and are also of interest to States and companies wishing to better protect their online databases.

The author of this book does not intend to propose a detailed technical approach of the different protocols and applications related to darknet here [REN 16]. It is not a computer manual either. The objective here is to deliver the keys to understanding a rapidly expanding phenomenon by defining the notions of the darknet, dark web and deep web by paying attention to the intellectual and ideological production that has accompanied and still accompanies the rise of alternative networks, in addition to examining the economic, security and geopolitical issues that are linked to the darknet (or deep web). Particularly, we will try to show that the clash between these different issues and between the diverging interests of users, institutions and economic operators always refers to the question of Internet governance modes. The darknets are on the threshold of a much more important era of development and make these questions crucial today because, as Peter Biddle, Paul England, Marcus Peinado and Bryan Willman asserted in 2003, "the genius of the darknet is indelible".

PART 1

New Frontiers and Governance of Digital Space

Fragmentation and Compartmentalization of Virtual Space

1.1. The nymph Carna and Internet census

One day, a computer scientist wondered how many Internet users could navigate this immense digital map, which is today's global network. Therefore, he created a small and perfectly harmless spy program named Carna Botnet, in honor of the nymph Carna, who became goddess of the *cardo*, the "hinge" or "axis", that is to say, the divinity of the gates in Roman rites, a charge that she inherited from the god Janus, who had taken her virginity in exchange.

> "The first day [of June] is consecrated to you, Carna, goddess of the hinges. She opens that which is closed, she closes that which is open; these are the attributes of her divinity"[1].

While Janus, honored on January 1, opens the first part of the year, Carna is celebrated on June 1, opening the second half of the year. The anonymous creator of Carna Botnet intimately knew her Latin letters. Carna is indeed a multifaceted goddess. If she was to be given tribute and sacrifice in June, the month in which the days were the longest, it was from her reign of the calendar that the period of the year begins, in which days begin to shorten until the end of summer and slowly turn into winter. The goddess of light, Carna is therefore also a goddess of darkness and concealment, or even a

---

1 Ovid, *Fasti*, VI, 107.

goddess of the underworld, with whom she is associated. This second attribute also makes her worth being considered as the goddess of organs and internal functioning of the human body, the "goddess of the human body viscera", so says the Latin author Macrobe[2].

From May to October 2012, the small program named after the goddess of entrails attempted to list all objects connected to the Internet with an IPv4[3] address. Out of a total of 4.3 billion IPv4 addresses available, Carna Botnet counted 1.3 billion active addresses in October 2012; 729 million occupied domains and 141 million addresses protected behind a firewall. In a previous "large Internet census" in 2006, 187 million visible users were counted. The latest estimates[4] put the total number of this era of smartphone users at just under four billion. Nevertheless, from his large "2012 Internet census", Carna Botnet's creator drew the conclusion that the development of IPv6[5] addresses might make any further census attempts in the future impossible. Five years on, in 2017, the growth of the connected objects industry and the ever-increasing number of users proved it right: it is impossible to know exactly how many users, devices, objects or servers are connected to the Internet today. Estimates and statistics continue to be produced, but remain doomed to be approximated.

It is therefore probably impossible to establish a precise geography of the global network today, and this can only be celebrated if we consider that the Internet must remain a virtual space in which privacy, anonymity and user freedom must be preserved. This libertarian concept contrasts with that of states and governments, striving to know and monitor cyberspace zones entrenched behind the barriers of encryption, or even more simply, lost in the ocean of data accumulated since the creation and privatization of the Internet. States are not alone in wanting to know about this *new terra incognita* of the digital universe, as private and public sector economic operators are also looking for ways to take advantage of them. In the face of various attempts at state regulation and commercial penetration of the "hidden Internet", communities and individuals are now trying to hide behind the supposed sanctity of encryption keys that allow, as way of an

---

2 Macrobe, *Saturnales*, I, 12, 31–33.

3 A 32-bit electronic identifier format, mainly used today on the Internet.

4 *EMC Digital Universe Infobrief*, research and synthesis accomplished by the *International Database Corporation* (IDC), April 2014.

5 A 128-bit electronic identifier format to replace IPv4.

example, two million users to surf the Internet anonymously using the Tor browser (The Onion Router), in the name of protecting privacy and freedoms, and sometimes for less admirable reasons.

The very provocative "Declaration of the Independence of Cyberspace"[6], issued in 1996 by John Perry Barlow, particularly resonates today. In Barlow's days, it was a protest against the Telecommunications Act that, according to the author of the "Declaration of Independence", supplied this virtual space of freedom (that is the Internet) to commercial appetites and the regulatory fury of companies and governments. But in 1996, the Internet was still in its infancy. Twenty years later, in 2017, we are not far off from considering that Barlow's wish came true. Cyberspace has somehow found its independence through its own extension and the phenomenon of encrypted networks. According to Campbell [CAM 07], author of a report for the European Parliament in 1997, the battle of cryptography was already lost by governments at the dawn of the 21st Century, which leaves room for the expansion of private networks and thus offers the prospect of a World Wide Web that is very difficult to control, a virtual territory largely beyond the reach of legislation; a gray zone between public and private space. The exponential growth of the global network, a vast web of networks and subnetworks numbering in the tens of thousands, in itself guarantees the relative powerlessness of States – which never had the extensive monitoring capabilities that they do today – from controlling Internet traffic. The mass of data represented by the circulation of these immaterial flows is impossible to process. Today, the Internet is simply too vast to be submitted in its entirety to the authority of regulatory bodies, or even to be comprehensively understood and apprehended.

1.2. Dimensions of cyberspace

There is a need for early comprehension on some definitions. The Internet is a global computer network composed of millions of public and private networks, made up of a set of sites, pages and databases accessible via the World Wide Web, invented in the early 1990s by CERN[7] computer scientists Tim Berners-Lee and Robert Cailliau. The World Wide Web is

---

6 See the text in the Appendix.

7 European Council for Nuclear Research, today known as the European Organization for Nuclear Research.

only one application among many (among others, the various e-mail systems and peer-to-peer file-sharing systems) that provides access to the Internet. The latter, since its official creation on January 1, 1983, and its opening to commercial exploitation in the 1990s, thus brings together an ever-increasing number of users, but also connected objects and databases, which can be accessed through browsers such as Google Chrome, Yahoo, Internet Explorer, Opera and other lesser-known browsers. According to internetlivestats.com, there were 3,611,467,000 network users on April 14, 2017 and 1,177,754,000 online sites. According to the same site, in April 2017, 2,580,768 e-mails were sent per second (including an overwhelming majority of spam sent by robots), 7,578 tweets, 776 photos uploaded to Instagram, 59,779 Google searches and 43,277 GB of data exchanged per second. In 2016, the International Communication Union estimated that less than half of the world's population had access to the global network. This leaves the Internet an impressive margin for growth.

This exponential growth seems to remove all significant issues on the size of the Internet. In July 2000, a study by Cyveillance, "Sizing the Internet" [MUR 00], estimated the size of the Internet to be more than 2 billion pages. Five years later, the strategic intelligence company DIGIMIND produced a study showing that the Internet had about 64 billion pages, while an Italian study announced in the same year that 11.5 billion pages were indexed by the main search engines. Nowadays, if we estimate the number of Websites created on the Internet at nearly 1 billion 200 million, it is very difficult to know how many active pages this can correspond to. In terms of data volume, the size of the Internet was therefore estimated at 4.4 zettabytes in 2014[8], equivalent to a number of digital tablets that would cover two-thirds of the distance from the Earth to the Moon, if they were end-to-end. The same study estimates that in 2020, the volume of data represented by the Internet will have exceeded 44 zettabytes, six times the distance from the Earth to the Moon, using the previous example. The rate of growth of the Internet now makes it possible to reach such orders of magnitude that we can now speak of a true "alchemy of multitudes", just as the researchers Francis Pisani and Dominique Piotet did [PIS 08, p. 188].

This "alchemy of multitudes", which brings together 4.4 zettabytes of data, nearly 50,000 different networks, 1 billion 200 million sites and an almost incalculable number of connected objects, constitutes the Internet,

---

8 Data Observatory, July 2014, op. cit., p. 8.

where the World Wide Web allows nearly 4 billion users to navigate. However, the vast majority of these users are unaware of most of these vast digital resources and will only visit a limited number of sites and pages that have been archived since the Internet was created. The most widely used search engines, such as Google and Yahoo, are supposed to reference at best only 15–20% of all content on the Internet, because of a number of restrictions that can be quickly outlined in the form of a table (see Table 1.1). These different types of content, which are indexed by search engines differently – or not at all – will determine the existence of subsets within the Internet, depending on the accessibility of online data and content. If we consider the Internet as a vast set of networks, where the application of the World Wide Web makes it possible to navigate and allows search engines to orientate themselves, from page to page or site to site, we will be able to distinguish several subsets that constitute the world web according to the different categories of contents.

Type of content	Description
Contextual content	Page content varies according to the context of access (e.g. e-mail homepage).
Dynamic content	Content hosted on a server, accessible by a request, whose display as a page is determined by a set of scripts controlled from the server. The user will access this type of page through a search engine. Dynamic pages are generated and controlled by an application from the hosting server (e.g. corporate or government Websites, or booking forms).
Static content	Page whose content is simply stored on a server database or online and made available on the World Wide Web via HTTP (HyperText Transfer Protocol).
Content with limited access	This type of content will not necessarily be encrypted, but search engine access will be limited by the use of anti-robot protocols (which will specify exclusion zones, but won't be necessarily respected by all automated search software) or CAPTCHA (Completely Automated Public Turing test to tell Computers and Humans Apart).

Non-HTML or non-indexable content	Specific formats not recognized by search engines. Flash content or using Javascript.
Private content	Password-protected content (typically: a private forum, e-mail, protected customer account, etc.).
Encrypted and protected content by application	Any type of content hosted on an alternative network such as Tor, I2P or Freenet. In this case, accessing it requires the installation of a specific software or search engine.
Orphan pages and archived content	The expression "orphan page" means a page that is no longer linked to another page or for which a search engine has been unable to locate the link. Archived content refers to all archived pages of a site, or even a site itself, that have become inaccessible to search engines.

Table 1.1. *Different types of content*

1.3. *Deep web*, *darknet* and *dark web*

The best thing to do with science today is to use it to explore the present. "Earth is today's alien planet", William Gibson said in an interview with the American channel CNN in 1997. Certainly, virtual space today is one of the most fascinating subjects of this unsettling terrestrial strangeness. Cyberspace is even the most faithful technical materialization of the Freudian *Unheimliche*. A virtual bottomless pit, a Pandora's box of fantasies, the Internet arouses the most imaginative theories in order to grasp the reality and complexity of the global network. One of the most popular today postulates the existence of "Mariana's Web", which would be the last level of the Internet, accessible only after a trip into digital darkness that has nothing to envy of the descent into the hells of Orpheus, all the way from level 1, frequented by M. The entire world, up to a kind of mythical plan containing almost all the secrets of the universe, from the manufacture of quantum computers to the location of Atlantis and the secrets of the Illuminati. Of course, this ultimate level of the Internet is supposed to be controlled by a mysterious secret society.

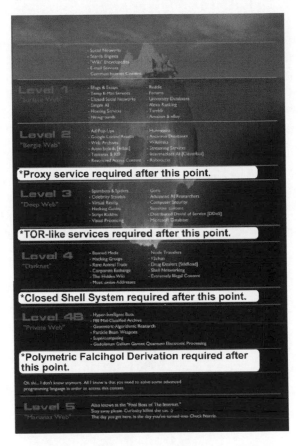

Figure 1.1. *The Internet in the form of an iceberg: a fantasy representation*

Another popular representation is that of the iceberg (Figure 1.1), which has the merit of offering a representation that is easy to grasp for the human mind: on the first level, the "surface web", and then the different levels of the "deep web" to the mysterious "darknet". The image, however convenient as it may be, is nevertheless based on a profoundly wrong apprehension of the division of virtual space. This division actually takes place according to the *accessibility* of content, as shown in Table 1.1: contextual, static, dynamic, limited and protected content. The volume of data also determines the ability of search engines to access data that is not necessarily protected, but simply poorly referenced or even impossible to reference. Therefore, in the vast entirety formed by the Internet, we can distinguish three subsets: the surface web, which can be accessed without any problems from simple queries on the most famous search engines, the deep web, a vast ensemble made up of non-indexed, private or difficult to access content and the darknet: the "hidden Internet", made up of various darknets, and alternative networks. Just as the World Wide Web is the application that makes it possible to navigate the Internet, dark webs are the subsets formed by sites and applications that make it possible to navigate, communicate and exchange on an alternative network.

Sites whose addresses ends with Onion are accessible via Tor (The Onion Router). Applications such as Grams or OnionCity (search engine on the darknet, see Figure 1.2) or sites such as TorShops or SheepMarketPlace (the latter being an alternative to Silk Road) are also part of the dark web.

Figure 1.2. *The Grams search engine*

We will then understand what distinguishes the deep web from the dark web: the latter does not even represent 0.005% of all the platforms present on the Internet. On the "classic" Internet, in other words the unencrypted and normally accessible without the help of a specific protocol or application, a forum such as 4Chan (Figure 1.3), which was widely publicized because of cases of hacking involved in US and French presidential campaigns, can provide a good example of data considered to belong to the deep web: it can be easily accessed by browsing through the forum, but a direct request on Google or Yahoo will not allow access to the content of the forum.

Figure 1.3. *www.4chan.org homepage*

If the Internet is a fantastic thread for all conspiracy theories, the darknet is an ideal fantasy object for the postmodern folklore of digital esotericism. The fascinating idea of a "hidden Internet" still leads to frequent confusion between darknet and deep web. The deep web, a term that could be translated as the "deep Internet", means nothing more than all the online databases, publications and archives that cannot be indexed by traditional search engines, due to the exponential growth of the global network since its creation in 1983 and privatization in 1994. According to the most recent studies, the "deep web" represents a volume of data 4,000–5,000 times bigger [CHE 17, pp. 26–38] than the surface web. The darknet, on the other hand, refers to a much more restricted part of the Internet whose access, contrary to the deep Internet, is regulated by very specific protocols and where, in contrast, legal regulations may not always apply according to the standards defined by law.

2

A Society of Control and Panopticism

According to cyber-activism theorists, the Internet is a space that should be beyond the control of States and major private operators. The reality today is, as we know, quite different, given that not only do States have the tools that make it relatively easy to trace the itinerary of an average user on the Internet, provided that the justice system is interested in him/her for one reason or another, but it is also obvious that personal data are collected as soon as made possible by companies for commercial purposes, often without the knowledge of users.

2.1. Horizontal panopticism and cyber-narcissism

As noted by the sociologist Borel [BOR 16], the communication society in which we live is a society of routine surveillance. However, this surveillance is not defined by a single model, be a vertical model of state control – Foucault's "biopower", or that of the Deleuzian "society of control". The different modes of controlling, monitoring and normativity of individuals are diverse and changing, adapting to the "liquid society" model defined in 2000 by the sociologist Zygmunt Bauman in *Liquid Times* [BAU 00]. Bauman's "liquid society" is opposed to the "solid society", whose structures and institutions are collective productions that guarantee the common good and the general interest. In this "liquid society", the only reference is the individual consumer, whose social status and identity are solely defined by individual choices and can therefore be subject to frequent and significant variations. Bauman thus defines social relations in today's society as increasingly impalpable. For Simon Borel, the nature of power exercised in networked societies, which can be compared to Bauman's "liquid society", is also changing and increasingly determined by the fact that distance relationships take precedence over interpersonal relationships. Thus, social control is exercised by different hierarchical structures, as well as by individuals themselves. The appearance of Web 2.0 and social networks has reinforced this trend by placing "self-employment" [DAR 09] at the heart of the postmodern mentality. To this, there is a pursuit for visibility, which is part of the "pathologies of democratic dynamics" [BOR 16]. This pursuit pushes individuals to seek the approval of their contemporaries and validate their social status by *likes* on Facebook, or by gaining more followers on Twitter or Instagram.

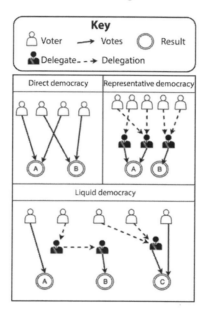

Figure 2.1. *Zygmunt Bauman's "liquid society"*[1]

Contrary to the original culture of the Internet, which prevailed from the late 1990s to the mid-2000s and which still makes the preservation of online anonymity a fairly common principle, the "Web 2.0", named after the appearance of the Internet of social networks, makes extroversion a marking feature of online sociability and social practices. In a virtual universe reshaped by GAFTA (Google, Amazon, Facebook, Twitter, Apple), a new form of panopticism would be "made up of a plethora of mirrors reflecting

1 Dominik Schiener, Medium.com.

image and identity" [BOR 16]. However, the search for visibility that characterizes some of the practices on Web 2.0 does not prevent the preservation of intimacy and privacy from becoming a priority, that is increasingly shared by network users, particularly after Edward Snowden's revelations and the threats to the neutrality and independence of the Internet.

2.2. The neutrality of the network in question

The democratization of Internet and World Wide Web usage from the late 1990s onwards generated a number of questions and claims as public use grew. For several years, the Internet remained in the public domain as a government-sponsored project and was then led by academic bodies. The simultaneous transition to commercialization as the explosion in the number of users has brought the Internet into a paradox that is difficult for it to emerge from today. What are the rules of governance that regulate cyberspace? Do governments have the possibility of legislating and exercising authority over the network, something that may have arisen from a state initiative, but which escaped this influence by the will of the American government? Can companies and enterprises that currently manage data hosting and Internet access claim any ownership rights over all or part of the network? Or does it represent a vast area of lawlessness, offering millions of users an area of preserved freedom in the face of the excessive amounts of control societies? Conversely, with the appearance of Web 2.0 and "horizontal panopticism", is not the Internet the most effective agent of this control society?

These are the queries that concern the development of the global network, as it grows and its own logic escapes its creators and users. The onset of alternative networks in the form of darknets paves the way for a new era, that we are tempted to call "Internet 3.0", as the computer tools and applications that characterize it have the capacity to overturn digital practices on a very large scale. More than ever, the Internet today simultaneously represents a formidable communication tool, a form of libertarian utopia, a surveillance tool and a legal enigma that is overall complicated by the development of encrypted networks.

In December 2015, Shari Steele, former director of the Electronic Frontier Foundation, took the lead in the Tor project, making no secret of her ambition to make the network a public instrument for the preservation of privacy and private life. For this "digital rights" activist, the large-scale development of the Tor project is essential to ensure that the Internet remains an area of freedom. For one of the members of the Tor project, whose pseudonym is Isis Lovecruft, the aim of this project is "to give everyone free access to information and to communicate their ideas. Without this possibility, the development of science and knowledge by humanity could decelerate or even stop" [LOV 16]. However, the paradox is that Shari Steele describes the organization supporting Tor as an "NGO (...) carried by a handful of brilliant engineers" [ROB 15]. Tor's new director readily acknowledges that much of the funding for the project comes from the US government [ETS 15]. The development of the Tor project presents the same contradictions and paradoxical situations as the development of the Internet. Initially, this is a project supported by academic bodies and benefits from government funding, more specifically, research projects funded by the US military or Navy. This does not mean that the development of the project is totally under the control of the military or the Navy, but it was clearly part of an institutional framework during the first years of its development, and was subsequently taken over by private and associative investors. This raises a simple question today: who is responsible for the Tor network and what is being exchanged? It is a burning issue, as Tor presents itself as an alternative network that is part of a logic of protest against public authorities, even though more than 80% of it is still being funded – as its founders and current director acknowledge – by the US government. However, the extension of the Tor network and the support given to the initiative by civil society and associative networks have taken the project out of the state's circle, while posing a serious threat to the US government, given that this it is possible to have this network create a virtual space that is beyond any state control. Tor's example shows how the development of darknets has complicated the development equation and collective control of the Internet since the privatization and democratization of the "network of networks".

The privatization of the Internet was widely initiated and regulated from the United States by the adoption of the 1996 Telecommunications Act under the Clinton administration, but the nature of the new space created by the Internet is, in fact, dualistic. First, it is necessary to distinguish between the physical architecture of the Internet made up of the physical network itself; in other words, the servers that host the data, and the wired and wireless networks that allow it to be transmitted. The Internet's "logical" architecture consists of all transfer and communication protocols allowing for data exchange over the network (Internet Protocol [IP], Transmission Control Protocol [TCP], HyperText Transfer Protocol [HTTP]). It is therefore only logical that the physical architecture, servers, wired, wireless and satellite networks were shared between private and public owners. Logical architecture, on the other hand, has always been open and without ownership, accessible to all, which is why the principle of net neutrality was founded and is now being debated and even threatened.

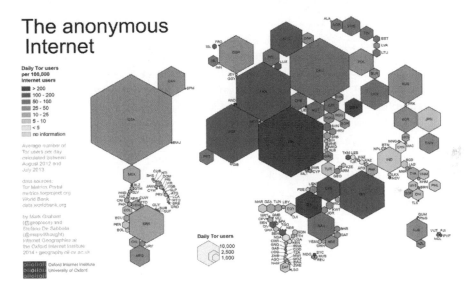

Figure 2.2. *Worldwide geography of the Tor network (source: Stefano Desabbata, Wikimedia Commons, August 23, 2014). For a color version of this figure, see www.iste.co.uk/gayard/darknet.zip*

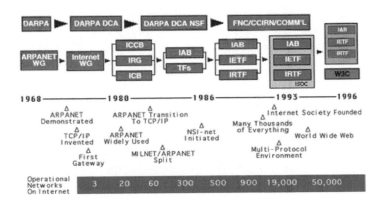

Figure 2.3. *Chronology of the first three decades that saw the emergence and development of ARPANET, which became the Internet (source: http://www.internetsociety.org)*

2.2.1. *How can network neutrality be preserved?*

"Communications regulators will invest more and more time over the next few decades in conflicts between private interests, represented by Internet service providers, and the public interest in a competitive and innovative environment centered on the Internet" [WU 03, p. 141]. This was acknowledged by American law professor Tim Wu in 2003, inventor of the term "Internet neutrality", who anticipated the emergence of a new field of conflict and legal expertise in a landmark article named "Network Neutrality, Broadband Discrimination". Wu's point can be summed up as follows: the promotion of "network neutrality" is no different from that which guarantees free competition in any private environment. In this area, government regulations intervene to ensure that the owner's short-term interests do not prevent the best products or applications from being available to users. It is therefore up to the American lawyer to "preserve Darwinian competition between the various possible uses of the Internet, in such a way that only the best survive" [WU 03, p. 142]. To do this, Wu considers three scenarios: (1) structural remedies, (2) a non-discriminatory regime and (3) self-regulation or non-regulation.

The structural remedy is open access (open source) to promote network innovations in favor of less intrusive models. However, Wu believes that open source itself is not enough to guarantee net neutrality. It is therefore possible to consider building a legal framework that protects the neutrality of the network. The principle of a network neutrality policy is to give users the right to (safely) use applications and the corresponding right for operators to produce them. Can this be guaranteed without regulation? Economic analysis suggests that operators have long-term interests that coincide with those of the public: both want a neutral environment conducive to the emergence of better applications. However, operators now appear to be less sensitive to these long-term interests and more inclined to favor short-term interests, resulting in an increase in conflicts over network neutrality. For example, operators have a tendency to ban innovations such as Wi-Fi or VPNs, for fear that they will lead to lower tariffs. These occasionally legitimate trends call into question the relevance of simple self-regulation in this area. Tim Wu therefore needs to clearly articulate the relationship between concepts such as open access, bandwidth discrimination and network neutrality. The latter concept implies belief in an innovation system, while the first two are the means to it. The article therefore aims to provide the theoretical model of a system based on network neutrality, an area in which users and operators are likely to oppose each other once the logical architecture of the Internet has been made accessible to all, without any centralized authority being able to favor a specific use of the network. For key players in the development of the global network such as Tim Berners-Lee, one of the inventors of the World Wide Web, this principle of opening the logical network is the best guarantee of the Internet's evolution and survival [BER 99, p. 99]:

> "On a conceptual level, if the web was destined to become a universal resource, it would have had to develop without hindrance. Technically, one centralized point of regulation was all it took for this to quickly become a constriction limiting web development, and the web would have never been developed".

Under these different approaches, network neutrality is therefore a principle according to which no private operator, being not only an access provider but also a service provider, can privilege its own users and products by means of tariff policies or technical measures aimed at favoring, degrading or blocking certain information flows to the detriment or benefit of others. Network neutrality is therefore a principle of equal treatment of all data flows, excluding any discrimination against the source, destination or content on economic or political grounds and for the purpose of restricting, exploiting or monitoring data exchanged.

2.2.2. *A threatened principle*

However, criticisms of the network's principle of neutrality, and even breaches of it, are increasing. The fight against piracy, the need to ensure bandwidth availability and the imperatives of cyber security are widely invoked to circumvent this principle. At the same time, the growing importance of GAFA[2] has given rise to fears that a massive privatization of the Internet will put a definitive end to the opening up of the global logical network and be taken over by large private groups and a capitalist concentration that would threaten, as has already been observed in other areas, freedom of use and innovation in favor of an economic model based on the preservation of short-term interests and profits.

---

2 Google, Amazon, Facebook, Apple.

"Google is currently creating a fully Google ecosystem, with its video subsidiary YouTube, the Google Wallet bank, Google Flights plane tickets... The precursor was Apple, which created a totally integrated model. The Internet, which presented itself as a horizontal universe and open to all, is being vertically restructured in silo, among just a few large operators. And all of them are American, none are European" [TAR 14].

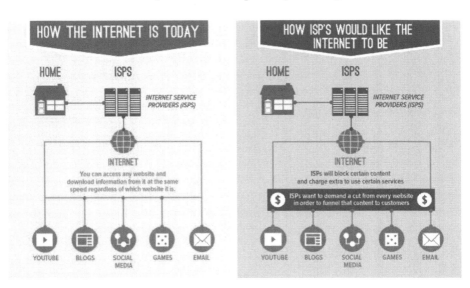

Figure 2.4. *Explanatory diagram of network neutrality*[3]

The privatization of the Internet is not a new issue. In 1998, Guillaume Duval asked himself in *Alternatives Économiques*: "No government, no parliament, no board of directors really decided to build a network of global networks. But now that the Internet is changing law, taxation and currency, the management of this infrastructure is becoming a central issue. Should we continue to let the Internet community reunite around the Internet Society (ISOC)?" The government's response was clearly negative, recalls the editor-in-chief of *Alternatives Économiques*, who puts forward a number of arguments justifying the Clinton administration's willingness to initiate privatization of the global network at the time: the inability of the Internet Society and the Internet Engineering Task Force (IETF) to continue

3 Sébastien Desbnoit, Internet&Moi.fr.

proposing a peer management model for the global network, the need to face the issue of global bandwidth congestion and the problem with the renewal of domain names.

Figure 2.5. *The Internet Society*

The Internet Society is an international association of American rights created in January 1992 by Internet pioneers in order to promote and coordinate the development of computer networks worldwide. In 2005, it was the most influential moral and technical authority in the world of the Internet.

Figure 2.6. *The Internet Engineering Task Force*

The IETF was created on January 16, 1986, initially composed of researchers and technicians responsible for managing the issue of technical standardization of the Internet. Although its activity was initially supported by the United States government, in 1993 it became a non-governmental organization whose activities were supported and supervised by the Internet Society.

In 1998, the United States was not willing to let their creation slip them so easily, emphasized in particular through Ira Magaziner, special adviser to Bill Clinton, that *the Internet having* "been developed as a project of the American government", its management would still legally be the responsibility of the Defense Advanced Research Project Agency (DARPA) [DUV 98]. At the time, this declaration provoked many negative reactions in the Internet community, but also tensions between Americans and Europeans over this highly sensitive issue. More than 15 years later, the tensions are still there. The French "law for a digital Republic", proposed by the

Secretary of State for Digital Affairs Axelle Lemaire and promulgated on October 7, 2016, known as the "Lemaire law", thus registered the principle of network neutrality as essential, a principle already defended in 2015 by Sébastien Soriano, President of the Communications Regulatory Authority, in these terms:

"We can imagine, that without Internet neutrality, an operator signs a contract with YouTube so that YouTube video traffic can flow more easily on to the networks, which would be to the detriment of Dailymotion, for example. (...) The Internet is a public space, which must be accessible to all under the same conditions"[4].

2.3. Going toward an Internet 3.0 and a new form of digital civility?

Can the Internet really be considered a public space, as Soriano describes it? The question arises in view of the network's origins, its use and exponential growth. Originally developed under the supervision of the U.S. government and the U.S. military, the Internet has become "internationalized", allowing states and communities, public and private companies and individuals to obtain IP addresses or domain names that enable them to exist and navigate the global "network of networks". However, in view of the development of alternative and encrypted networks, the question is even more important nowadays: what kind of governance could be adapted to the Internet, if at all possible today?

2.3.1. *Is cyberspace a public space?*

Public spaces are those that are frequented by the public regardless of their legal status, "private spaces open to a certain public, such as a shopping center or shopping mall" [PAQ 11, p. 3] and the expression covers very different and sometimes even irreconcilable realities, since the public space belongs to the legal, administrative and philosophical vocabulary, whereas public spaces "find their place in the glossary of edifices, engineers, urban planners, architects and more recently landscape designers". Public spaces thus refer to physical realities, often well delineated and localized, although

---

4 Sébastien Soriano, France Info, September 28, 2015.

public spaces are in no way limited to a geographical sense. The definition of public space also poses a problem in law, since the concept is essentially constructed by opposition to the private domain or private space. It is therefore the idea of ownership that comes into play when defining what belongs to the public space, but also the notion of use, which makes it possible to establish a certain number of rules and constraints imposed within a space considered as public, that is to say frequented by an indeterminate public since, if we refer to the definition given by sociologist Casillo [CAS 13], public space means "any space, in the physical but also virtual sense of the term, accessible to all and having the capacity to reflect the diversity of populations and functioning of an urban society". Public space therefore includes all the passageways and spaces of assembly open to all, which belong either to the State or to a private entity that has decided that this space is open to the public, or to no-one in particular. It is the *res publica* and *res nullius* of the Romans: the public thing, but also the "thing that belongs to no one in its own right". The definition applies to both public spaces in the plural – streets, squares, parks, etc., which are places of encounter and exchange – and to "public space" in the singular, a more abstract denomination that can sometimes be compared to "public sphere" or "public domain".

Public space is at the heart of democratic functioning. It is in the thesis of the German philosopher Jürgen Habermas, *L'Espace public. Archéologie de la publicité comme dimension constitutive de la société bourgeoise* (1962), that we find one of the most substantial attempts to define public space, which goes back to the historical roots of the notion, by placing it in the context of the *Ancien Régime*. Habermas then defines public space as the intermediary sphere that was historically formed between civil society and the State at the time of the Enlightenment. It is the place, accessible to all citizens, where an audience gathers to formulate a public opinion. The author thus calls public space "the intermediary sphere between the private life of each individual and the monarchical state, which is fond of secrecy, arbitrariness and denunciation" [HAB 93, p. 10].

Habermas reminds us that the word *public* was established in English from the middle of the 18th Century onwards, referring to advertising, in other words the fact of making public, but also public opinion and in many ways, a new form of common good, attached to the presence of intermediate locations between places of power and those of private life, where public opinion is formed more or less freely. "This public space allows private opinions to be made public, it includes lounges, Masonic lodges, academies, scholarly societies, philanthropic groups, clubs, cafés, newspapers, etc. When the press becomes independent of advertising, it can no longer play this role and this is the end of a certain public space", underlines researcher Thierry Paquot [PAQ 11, p. 10]. As Habermas also points out, the confrontation of opinions makes it possible to form a public opinion, and the "publicity" given to this opinion constitutes a means of pressure held by citizens to counterbalance the power of the State. But while the appearance of the communication society has led to an expansion and therefore to the standardization of opinion, and although an extreme diversification of channels of expression (which continues to guarantee the confrontation of opinions) can be observed, the public has split into specialist minorities, whereas the referee state continues to overstep its powers and ignore its limitations.

2.3.2. *Tyrannies of privacy*

Web 1.0, in which the act of communication was, in a certain manner, still based on the conception that characterized the salon society of the 18th Century, has given way to the new model of Web 2.0, in which the distinction between public and private has been blurred in favor of a vast confrontation and publicity of biases. The virtual social network has replaced the closed social space of the virtual salon where opinions were exchanged: Web 2.0 directly confronts individuals who are no longer necessarily emitters of opinion, but only of biases. However, if it is always in the public space that the *Self* experiences the *Other*, as Richard Sennett warned us in early 1979, in *Les tyrannies de l'intimité* [SEN 79, p. 202]: "The public man, who could play a wide repertoire of faces with the many masks that social situations attributed to him, is forced to limit himself to interpreting only one role, that of the private individual, thus depriving himself of an 'impersonal life'". For Sennett, in a society marked by the erased boundary between public and private, and faced with the temptation to seek refuge in microsociety or sheer subjectivity, civility becomes the primary societal value associated with anonymity [SEN 79, p. 202]:

> "Civility is the activity that protects me from other selves, and thus allows me to enjoy the company of others. The mask is the very essence of civility. The mask allows pure sociability, regardless of the subjective feelings of power, discomfort, etc.,

of those who wear them. Civility preserves the other from the weight of the self".

We must therefore understand here the essential issues, covered by the radical changes brought about by the development of the Internet to our social and societal model, and those that our society and the virtual space has created that are today intimately interwoven with our daily lives. In this sense, and if considered, after this historical and philosophical detour through the notion of public space, the very evolution of the notion of virtual space, we will understand how essential it is to define the nature of this virtual space and why it is debated so much. Is the Internet today a public space? Certainly, we would say yes, it constitutes this intermediary space between the private domain and the State, which is an emanation of civil society. By its very nature and history, the Internet belongs to the public domain, which means that its operation still largely depends on administrative decisions taken by institutions, that are in turn dependent on state authorities, in particular those of the Government of the United States of America. At the same time, the Internet is also the subject of a gradual privatization process that is giving rise to protests, hopes and concerns. The question of a development of an Internet 3.0, based on a new culture of anonymity preservation, and the development and increase in alternative networks partially escaping the rules enacted by state regulatory authorities or private law, is at the very heart of the issues that we want to expose here. In addition to the security, geopolitical and economic issues to which it is linked, the issue of defining the Internet as a public space raises crucial questions in terms of governance, individual rights and personal protection.

> "In this sense, we detect the obligation to exercise an administrative function of protecting public spaces that is independent of their classification and the status of public or private property. To this end, the administration competent in the regulation of the physical space may impose limits, use authoritarian powers to control and, if necessary, exercise police powers and administrative sanctions" [DIL 14].

It is therefore a question of the area of competence that must be applied to the management of the Internet, which can today clearly oppose States, private companies and representatives of civil society. This opposition materializes very concretely through the recent controversies and oppositions about the administration of domain names and electronic addressing on the global network. The development of alternative networks, known as darknets, and the stakes represented by the economic and scientific exploitation of deep web resources raise the issue even more acutely. As Mueller [MUE 17] points out, by its very nature, the Internet is a space that is fragmented by the multitude of networks it contains, but unified by the common language imposed by a universal protocol, TCP/IP. However, the Internet is above all a transnational space, deeply irreducible to the jurisdiction and logic of the nation state. The emergence of encrypted networks is not only inventing new data exchange and communication protocols, which are no longer dependent on the management of ICANN, but it contributes even more importantly to ensure that cyberspace is removed from state control.

3

The Internet, a Governance
Subject to Controversy

The emergence and development of encrypted networks further strengthens the Internet's capacity to withstand the pressure of states wishing to align the network or the constraints imposed by regulatory authorities, such as ICANN and the Internet Engineering Task Force (IETF). This makes the debate over Internet governance even more complex and vivid.

3.1. ICANN, an influenced institution

ICANN is an Internet regulatory authority based in the city of Los Angeles. ICANN is a company incorporated under California law, whose role is to manage the assignment of IP addresses and domain names. ICANN was created in 1998, after lengthy negotiations between Vice President Al Gore and the various actors involved in the development of the global network: researchers, industry, state government and administrative authorities. The agreement reached in 1998 gave ICANN the status of a non-profit organization, empowered in order to define addresses and protocol identifiers (TCP and IP addresses) and manage the system of generic and national domain names. It should be mentioned that a domain refers to a set of servers that can host and put online any data related to the same activity (for example, commercial), an institution, a State or an organization. To give a simple example, the .fr domain includes all individuals and organizations whose online activities are registered with the *Association française pour le nommage Internet en coopération* (AFNIC), an association that, for example, registers cultural and economic activities related to France. A domain name is therefore a unique address for a set of servers. The address of the encyclopedia Wikipedia is 208.80.154.224, but the domain name, which is certainly easier to remember, is wikipedia.org. ICANN's role is therefore pivotal, since it is this organization's work that allows Internet users to access the site of their choice, or find its name in a search engine, without having to type a long series of numbers.

3.1.1. *Is this the end of US supremacy?*

The allocation of domain names by ICANN was previously done under a contract with the U.S. federal government. However, this situation has been increasingly criticized over the years. ICANN's jurisdiction is *de facto* global and its decisions impose itself on other states, even though ICANN's statutes are defined by California law, which places ICANN under the authority of the Attorney General of California and the United States Department of Commerce. Thus, all changes to the .fr domain name must be approved by the U.S. Department of Commerce before they can be implemented. To put it plainly, all the domain names on the Internet depend on the goodwill of the California courts of justice and the American government.

Two factors have contributed to this development. First of all, Edward Snowden's revelations in June 2013, which triggered an earthquake in world public opinion that seriously shook the foundations of the agreement on which ICANN's status had been based until then. The brutal spotlight on the activities of the National Security Agency (NSA), and by extension the U.S. government, raised many voices in support of a comprehensive overhaul of ICANN's statutes in order to remove the attribution of domain names and IP addressing from what was perceived as an overly dangerous influence of the United States. ICANN Director Fadi Chehadé himself did not hesitate to argue on this point, prompting the U.S. government to consider abandoning its leadership role in favor of a kind of global governance of ICANN. However, the second factor of development was perhaps more decisive than the protests and petitions addressed to the U.S. government: on October 1, 2016, the contract between ICANN and the U.S. state expired.

Consequently, the 55th ICANN meeting held in Marrakech from March 5 to 10, 2016[1] was expected to result in the implementation of the transition

---

1 https://www.icann.org/news/blog/55e-reunion-de-l-icann-a-marrakech-temps-forts-de-la-session-de-la-division-des-domaines-mondiaux.

from Internet Assigned Numbers Authority (IANA) supervision, ICANN's department overseeing, in particular, the assignment of domain names and IP addresses of the Domain Name System (DNS). ICANN's reform was therefore supposed to free the Internet from the cumbersome American supervision. However, the validation of the plan from the Internet Corporation for Assigned Names and Numbers, after the Marrakech conference, raises new concerns that are expressed in particular by France, which strongly denounces the influence of GAFA lobbies (Google, Amazon, Facebook and Apple) in the negotiations of ICANN reform. This is not France's first clash with the Californian organization. Back in 2014, the French government, through French Secretary of State for Digital Affairs Axelle Lemaire, threatened to leave the international organization simply because ICANN had decided to sell the ".vin" and ".wine" extensions. The diplomatic crisis was narrowly averted and ICANN finally reversed its decision, but the French continued to demand that domain name management on the Internet be more neutral and that ICANN give more weight to the views expressed by the Governmental Advisory Committee (GAC).

3.1.2. *The role of the GAC*

The NSA's wiretap scandal, revealed by Edward Snowden, has accelerated the process leading to the establishment of true global Internet governance. However, the formation of the new GAC, with 171 members and 35 observers representing either national governments, or international or UN-affiliated organizations such as UNESCO, does not really satisfy those who denounced the control of U.S. government's and feared that it would be replaced by the GAFTA's major American companies.

Initially, the creation of the GAC was incorporated into ICANN bylaws to act as an advisory committee to ICANN's decision-making bodies. This is how the role of the GAC is described in Article VII, Section 3 of the ICANN Bylaws:

"A Governmental Advisory Committee will be established. The Chair of this Committee shall be appointed by the Board of Directors [N.D.A: of ICANN] and shall hold office until its successor is elected. (...) The members of the Governmental Advisory Committee shall be representatives of national governments, multinational governmental organizations, organizations created by international treaty, each entity being required to appoint one representative to the Committee. The Governmental Advisory Committee shall review and make recommendations on the activities of the Organization [N.D.A: ICANN] when they relate to the interests of governments"[2].

On the ICANN Website, the role of the GAC is defined as follows:

"The GAC is an advisory committee of ICANN, as defined in the ICANN Bylaws. It provides advice to ICANN on public policy decisions, particularly with respect to domain names (DNS). The GAC is not a decision-making body. It advises on issues that are within the scope of ICANN's jurisdiction. The GCC has a special status in the ICANN Bylaws. Its Board shall be given due consideration by the ICANN Board, and when the Board makes decisions contrary to the advice of the GCC, it shall provide the reason and attempt to reach a mutually agreed solution. (...) The GCC is an entity with multiple stakeholders and interest groups, in which governments must participate, as well as representatives of the domain name industry, technical development stakeholders, commercial and non-commercial users and representatives of civil society. The GCC was established in 1999, parallel to ICANN's first meeting, and has operated continuously since then".[3]

After the Marrakech meeting, the French Ministry of Foreign Affairs officially announced that it was feeling cheated, given the turn taken by discussions and decisions. "This is the privatization of ICANN, not its internationalization. The United States takes back with one hand what it gives with the other" [CHA 16]. The main reason for this concern is the unanimous voting process adopted to validate GAC opinions and communications, a process that risks giving much more overwhelming weight to representatives of private groups and interests, including GAFA. The U.S. side's main argument for the need for unanimity in decision making is the risk of undemocratic state representatives imposing their views

2 ICANN Bylaws effective from November 21, 1998. https://www.icann.org/resources/unthemed-pages/bylaws-1998-11-23-en.
3 "About the GAC", ICANN/GAC Website, https://gacweb.icann.org/display/gacweb/About+The+GAC.

on the GAC, with their sights focused at Russia and China. For Paris, this argument makes no sense since the GAC only has an advisory role. However, for the U.S. side, ICANN's bylaws make it very clear that any GAC advice requires clear justification and a consensual counterproposal before it can be ignored. The advisory role of the GAC is therefore sufficiently constraining to establish safeguards.

ICANN's reform and domain name allocation is shaping a geopolitical agenda that needs to be kept in mind in order to address the even more sensitive issue of developing and controlling alternative networks that are partially beyond the control of ICANN, governments and key players in the digital industry. On the one side, we see France benefiting from the internationalization of ICANN and the absolute preservation of network neutrality, supported by Argentina, African countries and parts of Europe, as well as China, Russia and Iran who want to give much greater power of control to States, while the other side sees the United Kingdom, Denmark and Sweden agreeing with the U.S. position of giving equal weight to both government and private sector representatives. In legal terms, it can be observed that in the debate between the supporters of a multiparty and joint GAC between representatives of States and the private sector, and those who defended the idea of a "United Nations Internet Organization" that are markedly more governmental and close to the organization of the United Nations Security Council, the dividing line is almost perfect between the supporters of the Anglo-Saxon *Common Law* and countries with a Roman-Civilist tradition, such as France or Latin America. The overrepresentation of Anglo-Saxons (States or companies) in the GAC constituted another point of friction. Despite the constitutional changes in September 2016 and the reform of the GAC, ICANN remains a California-based company that is outside the control of the U.S. government, but is in fact much more exposed to the influence of the infamous GAFTA.

Therefore, the issue of ICANN's change in status is absolutely crucial, given that it directly concerns the assignment of top-level domain names (a generic top-level domain [gTLD] is a type of domain maintained by the IANA. It designates the suffix at the end of a Website's address, such as .org, for example). With the issue of Internet neutrality, it can undoubtedly be affirmed that the independence of institutions for the allocation and regulation of domains is a determining factor in shaping the Internet of tomorrow. And it is not surprising that, apart from issues relating to ICANN's status, the Marrakech conferences and subsequent ones also dealt with cybersecurity issues, in addition to the increase in the number of domain names.

3.2. Cybersecurity, domains and electronic addressing

As French computer scientist Louis Pouzin reminds us, the American influence, or even control, of the Internet dates back to its creation in 1982 by a San Francisco team working on the first version of the DNS, a set of interconnected files serving as a directory. In 1998, after the death of Jon Postel, manager of this first DNS, ICANN was created to administer the "Domain Name System" in its stead. As representative of the Department of Commerce, ICANN also performs an economic function, an activity represented by Verisign, a private law company that manages the invoicing and extension of all domain names in .com and .net (80% of domain names on the Internet) for ICANN. To date, and despite the recent – and somewhat misleading – evolution of ICANN's status, the United States continues to exert a decisive influence on the management of the DNS. As Louis Pouzin reports: "In practice, the DNS has become indispensable. But its centralized structure is not essential. I often refer to the mobile phone. There are 1,500 to 2,000 operators around the world interrogating each other through a numbering system that is smarter than the Internet, based on a country and operator code"[4].

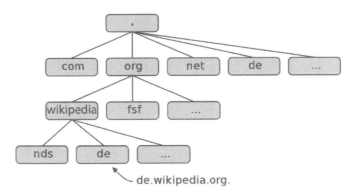

Figure 3.1. *Example of a DNS hierarchy (Creative Commons/Wikipedia).*
For a color version of this figure, see http://www.iste.co.uk/gayard/darknet.zip

---

4 Louis Pouzin is a French engineer born in 1931 and inventor of the datagram. His pioneering work has been used to develop the TCP/IP protocol. Interviewed in 2010 by Armel Forest for the *Club Parlementaire du Numérique*, http://www.eurolinc.eu/spip.php? article66.

Louis Pouzin, a former student of the *École Polytechnique* (class 1950), is an emblematic figure of computer science research in France, who was able to assist in the missed opportunity between French industry and the Internet, baring the consequences himself. After working for Bull and visiting MIT, Louis Pouzin became an engineer at *Météo France*, then at *Simca*. However, it is the fact that he took up office, alongside Maurice Allègre, at *Plan Calcul*, which allowed him to gain a wider knowledge of the technology developed in the United States, under the name of ARPANET. Recruited at INRIA (French Institution for Research in Computer Science and Automation) in the 1970s, he played a pivotal role in the development of the Cyclades project, aiming to develop a real interconnected network, similar to that developed in the United States by ARPANET engineers. Pouzin, in designing the datagram, even made a decisive technical breakthrough by designing the first packet-switched network. The administrative burdens, the lack of financial support granted to the project under the presidency of Valéry Giscard d'Estaing and the regrettable choices made by the French telecoms industry unfortunately sealed the fate of what could have become the French Internet:

> "Louis Pouzin, a polytechnic and very talented researcher (at the time) came to propose a project for a mesh network of computers based on something completely new: packet switching. Very quickly, the research was so successful that I made great efforts to have the project adopted by the Directorate-General for Telecommunications as the basis for their future data transmission network. Unfortunately, I hit a wall. (Telecom engineers preferred pushing the industrial development of *Minitel*.) We could have been among the pioneers of the Internet world (...). We are only users, far removed from the places where the future is being built"[5].

The decision not to give the Cyclades project team the means to continue its research obviously had heavy consequences for the French telecommunications industry, but also for the management and independence of the global network: "Everything that evokes a decentralization and internationalization of the directory arouses a strong mobilization of

---

5 Claude Allègre, quoted in: "Louis Pouzin: l'homme qui n'a pas inventé Internet", Stéphane Foucart, *Le Monde*, http://www.lemonde.fr/technologies/article/2006/08/04/louis-pouzin-l-homme-qui-n-a-pas-invente-internet_801052_651865.html, August 4, 2006.

American policies. Incidentally, we know a sociological reason for this reluctance: Americans believe that the Internet belongs to them. To bring up the DNS, is to enter their domain"[6]. The question of the "liberation" of the DNS and ICANN's emancipation from U.S. guardianship is not just linked to a question of selfishness and national pride. If we are mentioning these problems here, it is because the development of alternative networks exposes them in a much more radical way, and the regulatory authorities of the Internet are well aware of the security issues linked to these transformations.

> "There is then a simple political reason: DNS, thus designed, is an excellent means of observation. It is obviously impossible to observe everything that is happening. But by sampling, it is possible to examine the traffic of this or that user more precisely. It is a tool of economic intelligence. There is no formal evidence that it is currently being used for this purpose. However, a country that would have such a capacity and not use it would be foolish"[7].

In this instance, if the GAC members do not accurately reflect the interests represented by DNS control in these terms, the development of alternative solutions to the DNS represents a recurring or even pivotal subject of discussion and concern, particularly in the discussions around WHOIS.

3.2.1. *The essential role of WHOIS*

The WHOIS protocol (pronounced "who is", it is not an acronym) is an Internet protocol used to search databases (BDD) for information about the registration of a domain name or IP address. WHOIS was established in 1982, when the IETF published a protocol creating a master registry for ARPANET users. Originally, this register consisted of a simple contact list for users wishing to transmit data on ARPANET. As the Internet developed, WHOIS began to be used by different users, in addition to those already registered: legal authorities and police officers, trademark owners and beneficiaries of the Intellectual Property Code, individuals and professionals.

6 Louis Pouzin, interview mentioned above, Eurolinc 2010.
7 Louis Pouzin, *op. cit.*

When ICANN was established in 1998, it inherited the WHOIS protocol, as established by the IETF. On September 30, 2009, ICANN and the U.S. government signed the Affirmation of Commitments (AOC) that recognized ICANN as a private, independent and non-profit organization with the responsibility of ensuring public access to information provided by WHOIS, including registered users, registration fee information and administrative contacts. The AOC required this information to be regularly updated. From 1999, ICANN authorized other entities to offer domain name registration services. Responsible for maintaining TLD registration, ICANN has gradually redefined the consensus around WHOIS usage and operating policy, a set of rules specified in some key texts. Three of these texts are presented below:

– WHOIS Data Reminder Policy (WDRP): Implemented on March 27, 2003, it requires all users registered with ICANN to provide accurate and up-to-date information about the domain name they have registered with ICANN, as failure to do so may result in the deletion of the domain name concerned. The WDRP was implemented in virtue of ICANN's Board Resolution 03.41, following a vote by the Board of Directors on March 27, 2003. The Generic Names Supporting Organization (GNSO) is responsible for making recommendations to the ICANN Board on gTLD registration policy. The GNSO is composed of representatives of gTLD registries, gTLD subscribers, intellectual property rights advocates, access providers and representatives of commercial and non-commercial interests.

– Restored Name Accuracy Policy (2004): This provision specifies that if a registered domain has not provided the requested information, or if the information is incomplete, the domain name will remain in the process of being reactivatcd until such information is provided.

– WHOIS Marketing Restriction Policy (2004): This important provision establishes that domain name holders must ensure that no third party will use WHOIS information for commercial purposes and will also undertake not to trade in such information.

These statutes, which have remained unchanged for more than a decade, are subject to constant re-evaluation and debate within the ICANN institutions, as well as other entities involved in Internet governance and the Internet user community. The evolution of the Internet ecosystem is a real challenge in all areas: accuracy of information, access, compliance, privacy, abuse and fraud. The WHOIS structure is seen as increasingly inadequate for the evolution of the Internet. However, the replacement and substantial modification of WHOIS raises obvious technical, logistical and financial issues. As a result, ICANN has incorporated new standards for validating and verifying the data provided by domain name holders under the SSAV 38 report of February 25, 2009:

> "Parties identified as contacts for a domain name may be contacted for a variety of reasons, including general investigations (for commercial reason, for example), attempts to notify the holder of an incorrect DNS configuration and investigations regarding the possible involvement of the domain name in malicious, illegal or criminal activity. (…) Law enforcement agencies, computer emergency response teams (CERT), anti-phishing and anti-crime community (intervenors), companies that provide online reputation protection services, network operators, and Internet users may attempt to contact ICANN-accredited registrars when they are unable to communicate with a domain name holder using the contact information obtained from WHOIS services. (...) Public contact may only be available during specific business hours, whereas contact in the event of abuse should be available 24 hours a day, 7 days a week. Investigations involving suspected abuse or criminal activity usually require timely and even urgent responses"[8].

As a result, the SSAC recommended in 2009 that "registrars and retailers should assist in the investigation and mitigation of abuse and illegal activities". To do this, "each registrar would have to provide contact information in the event of abuse", the SSAC report specifying a "responsive and efficient" point of contact and the "person of contact in case of abuse" should "answer the phone and e-mail promptly", the contact details of these persons of contact being published on www.internic.net/regist.html.

In addition to this measure, ICANN's GNSO has produced a number of studies aimed at highlighting gaps in the WHOIS structure and the domain name registration process, including a report from May 23, 2013 categorizing, among other information, the modalities of domain names registration analyzed through a panel of 1,600 cases. Through this sample,

---

8 SSAC Recommendations 38, https://www.icann.org/en/system/files/files/sac-038-fr.pdf, February 25, 2009.

the WHOIS registrant identification study that was presented to ICANN by the University of Chicago's National Opinion Research Center determined the following distribution among ICANN-registered users to declare a domain name.

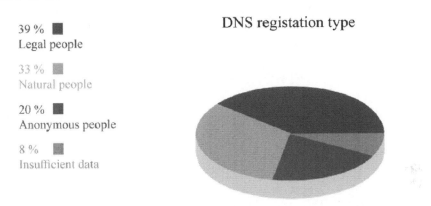

39 % ■
Legal people

33 % ■
Natural people

20 % ■
Anonymous people

8 %   ■
Insufficient data

DNS registation type

Figure 3.2. *The different types of domain name registration[9]. For a color version of this figure, see http://www.iste.co.uk/gayard/darknet.zip*

3.2.2. *Domain name extension and migration from IPv4 to IPv6*

Figure 3.3. *April Fools from http://com.google on April 1, 2015*

9 NORC/ICANN Study, 2013.

The issue of domain name assignment and control is crucial as ICANN approves the commercialization of new extensions. The development of the domain name market is being debated within institutions that still play a part in Internet governance and opposing States, users and private groups, with a number of governments denouncing the already established control of institutions such as large digital multinationals – notably the famous GAFTAs – over institutions such as ICANN and on the new domain name market. This process, which started in 2013, already allows local authorities to buy specific extensions such as .bzh for Britain and .paris for the city of Paris[10]. It also allows companies to create new extensions corresponding to their activity: .hotel for hotel owners, .shop or .google. Humorously enough, on April 1, 2015, the Mountain View company played an April Fool's prank on the Internet by celebrating ICANN's opening of a new generation of domain names.

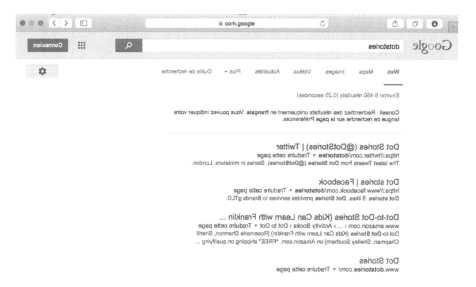

Figure 3.4. *The "inverted Google" of April 1, 2015*

In addition to the opening of new domain names, there is also the transition from IPv4 electronic addressing format to IPv6 format. The IP

---

10 See "Nouvelles extensions Internet: un nouveau Big Bang pour les domains", *Association française pour le nommage Internet en coopération* (AFNIC), thematic file no. 11, https://www.afnic.fr/fr/ressources/publications/dossiers-thematiques/nouvelles-extensions-internet-un-nouveau-big-bang-pour-les-noms-de-domaine.html.

address is the identification number assigned permanently or temporarily to each device connected to a computer network using the Internet Protocol.

"The IPv4 created in 1981 is capable of addressing 4 billion machines (2^{32}). Coded in 4-byte decimal place. Each byte can have a number from 0 to 255. Example: 192.177.5.2. IPv6 is the culmination of work initiated by the IETF to define a new electronic addressing protocol, established in 1998. It can support 3.4×10^{38} IP addresses (i.e. 3.4 × 1, 000, 000, 000, 000, 000, 000, 000, 000, 000, 000, 000, 000, 000). It is an address hexadecimal encoded in 16 bytes (8 parts divided into 4 parts of 2 bytes). Example: 3ac4:0567:0001:34b6:0020:0000: c7d7:4400".

IPv4 and IPv6 are incompatible without the use of a translation mechanism. This explains why in 2017, almost 20 years after its creation, the use of IPv6 is still limited to less than 10% of Internet users, while the IPv4 address pool has been exhausted since 2011 and can only be used for recycling, another problematic issue that has been on the agenda of ICANN's discussions.

3.3. Who regulates those who are in control?

The issues of the WHOIS reform and the opening of new domain name extensions were, among others, the focus of discussions that brought together representatives of States, user communities, international institutions and private companies working in the digital economy at the 55th ICANN Congress in Marrakech from March 5 to 10, 2016. This congress was followed by three other congresses: Helsinki, Finland, from June 27 to 30, 2016, Hyderabad, India, November 3 to 9, 2016, and Copenhagen, Denmark, March 11 to 16, 2017. Nevertheless, the Marrakech Summit was decisive in setting out the broad principles of the ICANN reform and the agenda for the subsequent congresses. It was during the Marrakech discussions that 76 members and 12 observers of the GAC set the framework for the ICANN transition announced by the U.S. government in 2014, and thus for Internet governance. The position of the U.S. Government was reaffirmed on this occasion in a very clear manner by Lawrence E. Strickling, Assistant Secretary of the U.S. Department of Commerce Assistant Secretary for Communications and Information:

"Since the inception of ICANN in 1998, the US government had believed that its role would be temporary. This week, the ICANN Board of Directors will transfer a proposal to the U.S. government. (...) We will not accept a transition proposal that would replace the NTIA with a government or an organization of governments. Secondly, the stability, security and resilience of the Internet must be maintained. Thirdly, it must meet the global expectations of customers, IANA's partners, and must also maintain the open nature of the Internet"[11].

3.3.1. *Conflict within ICANN*

The position thus expressed by Strickling aroused the concern of China, India and Russia, anxious to preserve the management capacity of governments in a highly changing context of the digital economy and politics, but above all, it met the frank opposition of France, Brazil and Argentina, who made it very clear that they disagreed with the ICANN reform proposal that gave governments only a very limited advisory and decision making role through the Government Advisory Committee, claiming only to have been able to provide non-binding advice to the ICANN Board, while representatives of the private sector, particularly the GAFTAs, seemed to be getting the lion's share within the governing institutions.

"Since the Internet has become global, this situation is no longer justified, which is why France has long advocated, and on several occasions, for the internationalization of ICANN. Unsurprisingly, in line with the concerns which it has repeatedly expressed and have not been taken into account, France is disappointed, seemingly like others, with the proposal presented despite a number of positive steps forward. (...) Whatever we say, States are marginalized within ICANN. In addition, States are not granted the same rights as other stakeholders in the mechanism of appeals, available to the community against decisions of the ICANN Board. Faced with this risk of jeopardizing ICANN's multi-party model, France, in accordance with its consistent positions reiterated in the minority declaration signed by nearly 20 countries, does not benefit from this reform, even though it wishes more than ever for the success of this transition, particularly taking into account the

11 Lawrence E. Strickling, statement made at the high-level government meeting with the GAC, 55th ICANN Congress, March 7, 2016.

objective of genuine diversity within ICANN and combating conflicts of interest. Throughout the reform process, France has worked constructively with others to try to reach a compromise, including the compromise proposed by Brazil at the Dublin meeting. This consensual compromise was entirely rejected by the CCWG, and I would conclude, Minister, that we cannot pretend to work towards consensus and ignore objections. France considers that this reform is disrupting ICANN's internal balances and once again undermines ICANN's multi-party model".

Box 3.1. *Statement by David Martinon, Ambassador for cyber diplomacy and the digital economy in France[12]*

The protest was officially reiterated, this time by the Brazilian government representative at the 57th ICANN meeting in Hyderabad, India, but no more than in Marrakech were the protesters able to change the course of the reform: in the new ICANN reformation, governments had to resign themselves to abandon a large part of the decision-making power to the private sector.

"These comments reflect the position of Brazil, Argentina, Chile, China, Colombia, France, Guinea, Paraguay, Peru, Portugal, Rwanda and Venezuela. (...) As a multiparty organization, ICANN must adopt and refine mechanisms that enable effective and meaningful participation of all sectors with an interest in coordinating and managing the unique identifiers of the Internet. (...) We firmly reject any solution that requires absolute consensus as a last resort, as it could lead to deliberations by the GAC to guarantee the right of veto to the various members of the GAC. With a total of 170 member governments, it would not be acceptable for one country to interfere with the decisions of all the others"[13].

Box 3.2. *Statement made by Brazil on November 9, 2016, on behalf of several governments at the meeting of the GAC at the 57th ICANN Congress in Hyderabad*

While discussions around ICANN's new statutes foreshadowed major developments in Internet geopolitics, the Marrakech Congress also

---

12 Statement made at the high-level government meeting with the GAC, 55th ICANN Congress, March 7, 2016.
13 Appendix 3 of the official statement of the 57th ICANN Congress, Hyderabad, India, November 3–9, 2016.

highlighted other concerns that were further elaborated by Ravi Shankar Prasad, India's Minister of Communication and Information Technology: "We value a free, open, pluralistic and inclusive Internet. Access to the Internet must never be discriminatory. It is therefore essential that we have access to this fantastic tool. Nevertheless, we must protect ourselves from cybercrime, dark web and other such problems"[14].

3.3.2. *Encrypted networks: a major security issue for ICANN*

The intervention of the Minister of Communication of India, a country with one billion mobile phones and 400 million Internet users, reminded participants of another reality: the emergence of alternative and even competing networks, whose development is not only capable of promoting the expansion of cybercrime to a level never before achieved, but also of disrupting the geopolitical nature of domain name allocation and electronic addressing at a time when ICANN, the main Internet governance institution, is undergoing a profound and controversial revision of its organization. The official statement of the Marrakech Congress concluded with an urgent call to regulate the use of proxies and private networks, and the 57th meeting of ICANN and GAC in Hyderabad reiterated the same urgent call to measure and control this phenomenon:

> "Malicious conduct from Internet domains does not take borders into account. Furthermore, the repression of such conduct must take into account the multi-jurisdictional nature of police investigations and operations they entail in order to protect the public, wherever they are being conducted. Hidden services are used to harbor perpetrators of malicious activity and to conceal other relevant information, rational mechanisms must be put in place in order to enable public safety authorities to uncover and obtain the necessary information to detect these malicious operators. We ask the P/P[15] working group to consider the need for judicial authorities to obtain information concealed by private services, so that they can continue to

14 Ravi Shankar Prasad, statement made at the high-level government meeting with the GAC, 55th ICANN Congress, March 7, 2016.
15 P/P: *Privacy and Proxy.*

protect the public from malicious conduct involving Internet domains"[16].

While an important round of negotiations is nearing its end to give a new form and framework to the institutional governance of the Internet, we are witnessing the rise of private networks in which Internet regulators are taking a keen interest, not only because they are promoting the development of cybercrime, as demonstrated by a recent Interpol report[17], but also because they directly threaten the fragile consensus between state and private operators on domain name management and electronic addressing. How can we define new standards and governance in this area when the increase of alternative networks makes it possible to set up and allocate domains and network addresses that cannot be referenced by ICANN or WHOIS, thus rendering part of its functions obsolete?

---

16 Official statement of the 57th ICANN and GAC Congress in Hyderabad, India, from November 2–9, 2016, Appendix A, GAC Public Safety Working Group (PSWG) comments to initial report (2008) on Proxy Privacy Accreditation issues.
17 https://www.interpol.int/Crime-areas/Cybercrime/The-threats.

PART 2

Crypto-Anarchism, Cryptography and Hidden Networks

To the crucial – and widely debated – question of network governance, the Internet community seems to have brought a form of non-institutional and drastic response, but nevertheless one that is part of the Internet's "natural" development logic. The exponential growth of the global "network of networks" puts into question, as discussed in the previous chapter, the "centralized" management model proposed since 1998 by ICANN. The commercialization of the Internet initially led the United States to relinquish part of its control over domain name allocation, due to the ambiguous legal nature of ICANN. The ongoing debates over the organization's new statutes illustrate the rivalry between the various operators claiming the legitimate right to participate in the administration of the network: States, companies, NGOs and user communities. However, these negotiations, which shape an Internet of a real geopolitical nature, only partially resolve the prickly issue posed to States and institutions by the logic of Internet decentralization and do not dispel doubts about the ability of regulatory institutions to enforce net neutrality in the face of massive digital industries, who now play an essential role in the functioning of these institutions. In summary, on the one hand, ICANN and some state and institutional operators see their inability to control the expansion of decentralized private or encrypted networks, and, on the other hand, the weight of GAFA and the network's monitoring capabilities developed by governments are urging part of the Internet community to encourage the development of an "out-of-control" Internet that has been dubbed as the 'darknet', in order to avoid a network that Barlow condemned 20 years ago in his "Declaration of Independence of Cyberspace".

In light of recent debates and technological developments, the future evolution of the Internet is moving in a direction that is difficult to describe. Is the appearance of a multispeed Internet, an evolution that would result from the massive privatization of the network, the development of IPv6 and also alternative networks such as Tor? Are these types of darknets, on the other hand, destined to be even more strictly monitored and controlled by governments and intelligence agencies because of the criminal activities that are taking place there? Or instead, will we really see a utopia of an alternative Internet transformed through cryptography into a basically lawless zone, while the "surface web" is delivered to the longing of GAFAs who do not hesitate to reconsider – for their own benefit – the neutrality of the net? Far from being reduced to mere havens of peace for hackers and criminals, darknets also convey an ideology and represent a model of decentralized organization that, without necessarily having the means to completely question it, are nevertheless opposed to the philosophy that currently guides the regulation of the Internet within international institutions.

4

From the ARPANET to the Darknet: When States Lose Cryptographic Warfare

The incredible expansion of global networking leads to a paradox: the reduction of real space, brought about by the unprecedented growth and modernization of the means of communication, is taking place alongside the practically indefinite expansion of virtual space shaping new and vast digital territories. While voyages of discovery have reduced *terra incognita* from the 16th Century onwards, the exponential development of intangible flows opens up new virtual *terra incognita*.

4.1. From Minitel to ARPANET

The end of the 1950s was historically marked by significant progress in telecommunications and advances in the field of information technology, which is still in its infancy. In France, it is the engineers of the *Centre national d'études des télécommunications* who continued research in this field, in collaboration with the researchers of the *Plan Calcul*, launched in 1966 under the impulse of President Charles de Gaulle and his Minister of Economy and Finance (and former Prime Minister) Michel Debré. The competition between developed countries was harsh between French, British, Germans, Russians and Americans, who embarked on a race that would not only lead to the advent of "personal computers" in homes, but also to the birth of the Internet. This project was developed under the aegis of the United States' DARPA, while the French were simultaneously working on the Minitel project (interactive media by digitization of telephone information), developed in Rennes by the Center for Television and Telecommunications Studies, under the direction of Bernard Marty and the supervision of Jean-Paul Maury, the first prototypes of which were tested in 1977.

The Minitel had several competitors: the British had taken an interest in videotext technology with the Ceefax system that was launched in 1972 (then with Prestel in 1979), and the United States had developed the NAPLPS system (North American Presentation-Level-Protocol Syntax). However, the NAPLPS had a major disadvantage: the near-photographic quality of its videotext display technology, which could have been seen as an advantage, was actually a disadvantage for a low-bandwidth data transmission protocol. The Germans, on their side, designed a telecommunications service that was much closer to the Minitel, which was able to offer a wide range of online services, comparable to those offered today on the Internet. Nevertheless, the German *Bildschirmtext* was a commercial failure, mainly due to the prohibitive cost of equipment. By the time the German postal services, who were in a monopoly situation, realized that it was necessary to lower tariffs in an attempt to save *Bildschirmtext*, Amiga, Atari, Amstrad and IBM's first PCs had already begun spreading into households.

The appearance of the first models of personal computers, produced by IBM, Commodore, Sinclair and Apple in the early 1980s, coincided with the success of American researchers and academics' work with ARPANET. The debate is still raging today about the real influence of Minitel on the development of the Internet. Like their German counterparts, French policy makers have not been able to take advantage of the technological and commercial advances they had initiated. The Americans were largely interested in the development of Minitel, and it was not so much the techniques used, but the content and services offered that generated interest across the Channel: Minitel not only offered the user the possibility of having access to a large online database and a wide variety of services, but also to a large online community, in which it was possible to establish real exchanges. The use of Minitel by student protesters, to coordinate their actions against the Devaquet reform in 1986, preceded the role of the Internet in the Arab revolutions by 25 years. The scale is obviously not the same, but the phenomenon of acting through an online community was already there and foreshadows what would constitute the very nature of the Internet, creating a global community of users, of which very varied conditions of expression and exchange can be found today in the social networks of the web 2.0 and alternative networks of Internet 3.0.

4.1.1. *Rapid growth*

ARPANET, the forerunner of the current Internet, was a university project funded by a branch of the army (Advanced Research Projects Agency (ARPA)). Initially, the network only connected the University of Utah and three Californian research centers. ARPANET was the forerunner of the modern "packet" sending technique, in other words the fragmentation of data into "packets" that are easier to transport over a network. One of ARPANET's first applications was Telnet, which allowed a researcher to connect with the computer workstation of another site. By the late 1970s, ARPANET had seven communication nodes, including MIT and Harvard. Each ARPANET site had a router costing $82,200, or half a million dollars today. In 1973, ARPANET became international, because of a satellite connection linking Norway, London and Hawaii to the American nodes. The network then expanded to 40 nodes. E-mail was invented in 1971 by an engineer named Ray Tomlinson, who also invented the "@" in e-mail addresses. The File Transfer Protocol was developed, allowing ARPANET to exchange files as data packets. This was around the same time that asymmetric key encryption was being developed. This invention arised from a simple technical problem: the saturation of telephone networks from the 1960s onwards forced the army itself to manage an ever-increasing number of digital keys for a growing number of users. So, it was in 1976, at Stanford University, that Whitfield Diffie and Martin Hellman theorized the first real key distribution system on a computer network, giving rise to what was later called *telecommunications*. The idea was simple and still lies at the heart of encrypted networks such as Tor: both the sender of a message and its recipient can encrypt the message using an encoding key and a decoding key.

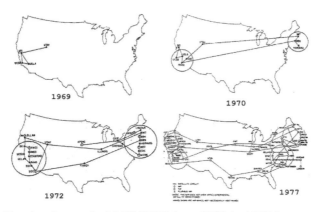

Figure 4.1. *The development of ARPANET from 1969 to 1977 (source: Wikipedia)*

4.1.2. *The privatization of the Internet*

Originally, ARPANET was managed by the military. However, the designers realized that the network could not remain centralized if it continued to grow. Different networks had to be created, controlled by different organizations and using a common standard. This is precisely what the French never decided to do with Minitel, an excellent centralized system. At the World Open Source Software Meeting in Amiens on Friday, July 13, 2007, Benjamin Bayart proposed to name the process of centralizing the Internet, and the web in particular, "Minitel 2.0". According to him, this trend toward centralization, which undermines the network's neutrality and restricts the potential of its players, brings the Internet and Minitel together: a totally centralized system in which it is necessary to apply for authorization to transmit and where reception is the norm. At any rate, in the early 1980s, the U.S. Army commissioned two engineers, Vinton G. Cerf and Bob Kahn, to design a new standard for communication and data packet exchange: TCP/IP, TCP (Transmission Control Protocol) and IP (Internet Protocol) was adopted by ARPANET on January 1, 1983, marking the birth of the Internet. Another network, CSNET, founded by the National Science Foundation, connected to ARPANET using the TCP/IP protocol. When ARPANET was deactivated in 1990, it only had a mere 40,000 Internet constituents on its network. In the 1980s, the National Science Network created a TCP/IP network called NSFNET, linking several supercomputer-equipped centers. The speed and flow rate of this network led others to try and connect to NSFNET, making it the first backbone of the Internet. In 1992, 6,000 different networks were connected, a third of them overseas, because of an application developed that year called the *World Wide Web*. Internet marketing had begun. In 1994, the Clinton administration privatized the backbone. NSFNET passed the baton to private companies in charge of handling long-distance communications. The U.S. government was anxious not to create a monopoly situation by sharing the cake between different companies: UUNet (now Verizon since 2006), AT&T, Sprint and Level (3).

As the authors of a major report by the International Institute for Strategic Studies (IISS) published in March 2016 [MOO 16, pp. 7–38] recall, political decisions in the field of cryptography test the values of liberal democracy in the 21st Century. Democratic governments face an almost impossible dilemma: should the protection offered to citizens and Internet users be called into question, by depriving them of the right to protect their data and privacy, in order to prevent individuals engaged in criminal and unlawful activities from benefiting from the same protection? Today, cryptography is directly linked to the two major threats of terrorism and the criminal exploitation of IT flaws, but data encryption is also a technical possibility that fully participates in the development of the Internet and guarantees net neutrality in the same way as the decentralization of the Internet. However, should governments not seek to limit the very rapid development of computer encryption techniques? The development of telecommunications made this question an essential issue very early on.

4.2. The rise of asymmetric cryptography

At the dawn of the 1960s, with the development of communication networks and the significant increase in the number of users, the very real problem of limiting the number of identification keys available began to arise, particularly for armed forces, faced with the problem of maintaining secure radio connections, despite the increase in communication channels and the saturation of radio frequencies. James Ellis, an engineer and mathematician at the GCHQ (Government Communications Headquarters), began to work on the issue of public key encryption, well before the same problem was raised some 10 years later, in the field of computer network communication, by Whitfield Diffie, Martin Hellman and Ralph C. Merkle, all three of whom were researchers and cryptologists at Stanford University [DIF 76, p. 644]: "The cost and delay imposed by this key distribution problem is a major obstacle to the transfer of the communications market to large teleprocessing networks".

4.2.1. Steganography

Cryptography, recalls economist and computer scientist Jean-Philippe Rennard [REN 16, p. 30], is "the study of the processes of representation of messages, so that they are only understandable by the recipient(s)". Cryptography is an extremely ancient technique. The first historical examples date back to the "Kahn Encryption", named after the historian who identified this method used by an Egyptian scribe in 19th Century BC, and in 16th Century AC, as evidenced by a tablet of clay found in Iraq, on which a Mesopotamian potter detailed his pottery technique, while taking care to alter the spelling of words and the meaning of the message so that it was understandable only by himself. Cryptology, which literally means "the science of secrecy", became an academic discipline in the 1970s and distinguishes two main methods of concealing a message: cryptography and steganography. The first consists of rendering a message incomprehensible by means of a key, that is to say, by means of a particular method, which once known, makes it possible to decipher the message. The second, from the ancient Greek στεγανός/steganós ("impermeable") and γραφή/graphé ("writing"), consists of concealing one message in another.

Figure 4.2. *An example of a stenographic message [LED 96]. Drawing with a hidden message. The message is coded in Morse code in the long and short grasses on the river bank. A long grass is a line, a short grass is a point. The message reads: Compliments of CPSA MA to out Col Harold R. Shaw on visit to San Antonio May 11, 1945.*

Herodotus reports how Demarate, former king of Sparta, was able to warn his former homeland of the invasion plan instigated by the king of Persia because of a tablet carrying a message engraved in the wood, covered with wax to make it look like a tablet of virgin wax, or even how Histiee, tyrant of Miletus, carried out secret orders tattooed on the skulls of slaves.

One of the most famous uses of steganography, however, is the very sharp epistolary exchange attributed to George Sand and Alfred de Musset, who maintained an intense relationship between 1833 and 1834. If the authenticity of the exchange is called into question, the steganographic process is exemplary and we will leave it here for the reader to discover it... and understand the meaning of the messages supposedly exchanged by the two writers:

Letter from George Sand to Alfred de Musset:
I'm very moved to tell you that I have
well understood the other night you were having
always had a crazy urge to be
dancing. I keep the memory of your
screwed and I'd like it to be
this is proof that I can be loved
by you. I'm ready to show you my
disinterested and without cal-
arse, and if you want to see me
unveil my soul to you without artifice
naked, come and visit me.
We'll talk as friends, frankly.
I'll prove to you that I am
sincere, capable of offering you affection
the deepest as well as the tightest
in friendship, in a word the best proof
woman that you can dream of, since your
soul is free. Think the loneliness where I ha-
cock is very long, very hard and often
difficult. So, when I think about it, I have the soul
big. Why don't you hurry up and put it
to make forget by the love where I want to be
in me.

Answer from Alfred de Musset to George Sand:
When I put an eternal tribute at your feet
Would you like me to change my face for a moment?
You captured the feelings of a heart
That to worship you formed the Creator.
I cherish you, love, and my feather is delirious.
Lay on paper what I dare not say.
With care, from my verses read the first few words
You will know what remedy to bring to my ailments.

Reply from George Sand:
This insignia that your court is asking for
Night my fame and disgust my soul[1].

---

1 The decoding is kindly submitted by the site: http://5ko.free.fr/fr/sand.html.

4.2.2. *Modern cryptographic methods*

With the assistance of machines, modern cryptography made significant progress during the Second World War. The "Lorenz machine", developed by the Germans during the war, was able to transmit encrypted messages using the Baudot code. This type of perforated ribbon coding, developed by Émile Baudot in 1874, is based on a binary code and the Latin alphabet, each character being coded with a series of 5 bits (0 or 1) to obtain 32 combinations. The Baudot code was the first mechanized character coding in history.

Lorenz's machines are less well known than the famous Enigma machines that were used to encrypt the German army's communications, but they transmitted messages of great importance since they were used to encrypt communications between headquarters, staff headquarters and the highest levels of decision-making within the Nazi unit, thus making it possible to transmit "encrypted attachments" between these various decision-making bodies, as indicated by their administrative names "SZ 40" and "SZ 42" (for "Schlüsselzusatz", which means "encrypted attachment").

On August 30, 1941, an error made by a German operator allowed the cryptanalysts at Bletchley Park in the United Kingdom to intercept two messages sent back with the same encryption key, which made it possible to understand how Lorenz's machines worked. In order to decipher German communications more quickly, the British developed the Colossus computer, which can be considered as the world's first digital electronic computer. The computer decryption of the communications carried out by Lorenz's machines, and that of the transmissions carried out by the German army using the Enigma machine, a decryption made possible by Alan Turing's work on the basis of information transmitted by the French and Polish intelligence services, marked the beginning of the era of cryptography and modern cryptographic wars.

Symmetric cryptography can indeed be distinguished from asymmetric cryptography, which is much more recent. Symmetric cryptography is based on the principle of a decryption key for a message that is owned by both the sender and recipient of the message and can thus be decrypted by means of the key known in advance. According to the rule established by the Dutch cryptologist Auguste Kerckhoffs, in his work *La cryptographie militaire* (1883) [KER 83], symmetrical cryptography is based on the principle of disclosure of the key by the sender of the message to a third party and on "computational security", in other words the decryption of the key requires too much computing power to be possessed by a third party wishing to possess it. Technological progress, particularly in the field of computer science, has greatly undermined this "computational security" and more recent cryptographic work has paved the way for asymmetric cryptography, which is now used in the encryption of data on the Internet.

4.2.3. *Asymmetric cryptography*

Asymmetric cryptography is the result of much more recent work. It is based on the use of two encryption keys, whereas symmetrical cryptography only uses one: a key used by the user to "encrypt" the message they send, in other words make it unintelligible by a third party, and a decryption key that will allow the recipient to decrypt the message. In this case, the encryption key is public, while the recipient uses a private key to decrypt the message. Nowadays, this type of encryption is used in registered electronic letters, electronic passports, website user authentication, electronic safes, for the electronic signature of documents and the so-called "asymmetric" algorithm of the RSA, designed by Ron Rivest, Adi Shamir and Leonard Adleman, which is based on a simple method:

"Message encryption: $c = m^e \bmod n$

Message decryption: $m = c^d \bmod n$

In these two operations: m denotes the unencrypted message, c denotes the encrypted message, (e, n) the public key, (d, n) the private key, n denotes the product of two prime numbers, $^\wedge$ denotes the power operation (m power e) and mod is the modulo operation which allows to determine the rest of the entire division.

To make it easier to understand the models used in asymmetric encryption, cryptography uses the characters "Alice" and "Bob", created by Ron Rivest in an article published in 1978, detailing the mechanism of the RSA encryption system [RIV 78, pp. 120–126]. In their article, Rivest, Shamir and Adleman describe the following operators: "For our scenario, we assume that A and B (also known as Alice and Bob) are two users of a public cryptosystem key" [RIV 78, p. 121]. Alice and Bob's characters are used as reference figures in cryptography, but also in fields as varied as game theory, physics, quantum cryptography or to solve complex problems such as predicting heads or tails over the phone [BLU 83a, pp. 23–27]. Over the years, engineers and researchers using Alice and Bob to illustrate their research have sometimes even had fun giving Alice and Bob a somewhat richer personality and biography. In 1983, Blum even imagined a troubling past for Alice and Bob: "Alice and Bob, recently divorced and conversely distrustful, continue to do business together. They each live on an opposite coast, communicate mainly by telephone and use their computers to conduct transactions over the phone" [BLU 83b, pp. 175–193].

The cryptographic war did not end in Bletchley Park after the Second World War, and the friendly Alice and Bob were even seen as dangerous enemies of the state as, in the 1970s, research by cryptologists such as James Ellis of the GCHQ, Whitfield Diffie, Martin Hellman and Ralph C. Merkle of Stanford, brought data encryption out of the military domain and gave civilian cryptography a decisive push.

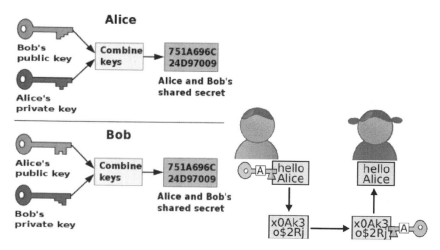

Figure 4.3. *The adventures of Alice and Bob. For a color version of this figure, see www.iste.co.uk/gayard/darknet.zip*

The rise of civil cryptography was indeed initiated, as we explained earlier, by the problem of key distribution – in the sense of a digital value, allowing to identify a user on a network – a problem which, first and foremost, concerned wireless radio communications and prompted James Ellis' pioneering work at the GCHQ. When the same problem arose for telecommunications between computer networks, Whitfield Diffie and Martin Hellman devised a simple solution: there is no reason why only the sender of a message can encrypt it, the recipient can also take part in encryption. This revolutionary idea was the attested dawn of asymmetric cryptography, with the publication of Whitfield and Hellman's work in 1976, until 2 years later, Rivers, Shamir and Adleman created the RSA – the principle of electronic signature – and Merkle in turn published seminal work for the advancement of asymmetric cryptography, soon adapted to a new form of electronic communication, of which Rivest, Shamir and Adleman were able to perceive its emergence in a visionary manner [RIV 78, p. 120]: "We will soon be entering the era of 'e-mail'. We need to ensure that two important properties of 'paper mail' are preserved: messages are private and messages can be signed". This revolutionary assertion, which may seem mundane today, was to be the only theoretical basis for, on the one hand, the confrontation between governments and intelligence agencies, and, on the other hand, communities of users and private operators, an opposition that still exists today, 4 years after the Snowden case, when darknets are booming.

For if Rivers, Shamir and Adleman presented in their article the first two properties of electronic exchanges that asymmetric cryptography was able to preserve, then the researcher David Chaum would be the one to have given substance to a third property that states view even more negatively: anonymity. In 1981, Chaum, a young 26-year-old mathematician from the University of California at Berkeley, created a cryptographic method to counteract attempts at traffic analysis and make the user anonymous, not by deleting his e-mail address (that is to say his public identification key), but by disguising it under several layers of encryption. Chaum had just formulated the idea that would serve as a basis for .onion routing. David Chaum was well aware of the political implications of his finding and was already critically analyzing the consequences of the digital revolution [CHA 85, p. 1,030]: "The foundations of a "records company" are questioned, in that computers can be used to influence lifestyles, clothing choices, habits, movements and associations based on data collected during transactions made by ordinary consumers".

4.3. "The Crypto Wars are over!"[2]

"Signal espionage organizations recognize that the long battle against civil and commercial cryptography has been lost. A strong academic and industrial community is now well versed in cryptography and cryptology. The Internet and the global market have created a free flow of information, systems and software. The NSA failed in its mission to maintain access by claiming that the "key depository" and similar systems were intended to meet the needs of the police (rather than those from COMINT organizations). Recognizing this, the United States liberalized its encryption export regime in January 2000, allowing citizens and non-U.S. companies to buy and use powerful encryption products" [CAM 07, p. 112].

The conflicts of the early 20th Century shaped modern signal interception techniques and the first proven signal interception companies were credited to the British Royal Navy during the Boer War (1899–1902) and the Sino-Japanese War (1904–1905) during which one of Her Majesty's ships, the *HMS Diana*, managed to intercept the Russian radio signal calling for the mobilization of its fleet. The First World War further developed these techniques. The German Schlieffen plan for the invasion of France was discovered, in part, because of the efforts of the French Chiffre Service and British intelligence, and the efforts of the French crypto analyst Georges Painvin at the end of the war, who made it possible to break the German code ADFGVX and prevent the counterattack launched in spring 1918 by the German forces. The British in particular deployed a formidable intelligence and signal interception strategy. At the beginning of the war, thanks to the Royal Navy's mastery of the seas, they managed to cut all the transatlantic cables used by the Germans, forcing them to use telegraph lines... connected to the British network and on which it was easy to spy on communications.

Continuous technical development has made signal interception and electronic intelligence a major field of modern warfare, now divided into multiple areas of activity and data collection. SIGINT/HUMINT acronyms began to be used during the Second World War. COMINT, ELINT, IMINT, etc. would make their appearance later, with the evolution of

---

2 "The Crypto Wars Are Over!", FIPR, available at: http://www.fipr.org/press/050525crypto. html, May 25, 2005.

telecommunications and surveillance techniques, which would make it possible to widen the field of intelligence considerably.

Acronym	Meaning
HUMINT	HUMan INTelligence: human intelligence, social engineering
SIGINT	SIGnal INTelligence
COMINT	COMmunications INTelligence: interception and interpretation of communication channels and flows
ELINT	Electronic INTelligence
ECINT	EConomic INTelligence
IMINT	IMagery INTelligence: interpretation of satellite imagery
ACCINT	ACCounting INTelligence: accounting information
GEOINT	GEOspatial INTelligence: study of human activity on the Earth's surface from maps, satellite imagery, geospatial and geodetic sources
LOCINT	LOCation INTelligence: monitoring and tracking from mobile telecommunication devices (telephone, laptop computers, etc.)
MASINT	Measurement And Signature INTelligence: a branch of intelligence consisting of identifying any type of signature: radioactive, radio, biochemical or biological
DIGINT	DIGital INTelligence
OSINT	Open Source INTelligence: public access data collection: media, Internet, etc.
SOCMINT	SOCial Media INTelligence: monitoring and analysis of social networks
PROTINT	PROtected information INTelligence: collection of information from protected databases

Table 4.1. *The different types of information and data collection [OMA 12]*

COMINT, ELINT, DIGINT, SOCMINT and PROTINT are intelligence branches whose resources are particularly dedicated to monitoring the Internet network and collecting information on the web surface, the deep web and encrypted networks such as darknets. Over the past 20 years,

COMINT and PROTINT have been branches of intelligence particularly involved in what specialists and the media have called "cryptographic wars". The advances made, because of the work of Whitfield, Hellman, Merkle and Rivers, Shamir and Adleman in the 1970s, initiated a confrontation between intelligence agencies and civil society, which was taken on by full force from the 1990s onwards, with the opening of the Internet to the general public. However, it was David Chaum's work that fanned the flames.

4.3.1. *Planetary electronic monitoring*

The development of digital technologies has changed the structure and techniques of intelligence, just as much as those of the advertising industry. The intensification of digital usage and the rise of electronic messaging on social networks has encouraged the appearance of Chaum's "records company" in 1985: a society in which IT and digital tools ensure the traceability and efficient filing of individuals in order to influence their consumption patterns and set up an effective police surveillance system.

> "As a result, developers, programmers and publishers who depended on the advertising industry have been tempted, if not obligated, to create an infrastructure that would slavishly serve as a means of monitoring individual transactions on the web. The restructuring and budgeting of the advertising industry, in addition to the rising value of information about commercial interests, is leading to the emergence of a web-based infrastructure that would serve to monitor the interests of those involved in its creation. By the early 1990s, private and libertarian innovators had begun to get unsettled by this concerning flaw in the growing web, and more particularly by its growing propensity to violate laws protecting privacy and individual rights" [CHR 15, p. 3].

With the appearance, and particularly the opening up and commercialization of the Internet, public authorities, governments and state intelligence agencies very quickly saw the emergence of a new and vast field of information gathering because of digital tools. In 1997, in the report prepared for the European Parliament's Office for the Science and Technology Options Assessment (STOA), Scottish journalist and researcher Duncan Campbell described in great detail the extent of the surveillance system implemented by the American NSA and the British GCHQ for the Internet, among other communications networks. As early as the 1980s, says Campbell, the NSA and its UKUSA[3] partners were operating an international communications network that was larger than the Internet at the time, a sort of early darknet, a Global Wide Area Network (GWAN), an extensive global network representing an international digital surveillance structure. In the 1990s, COMINT systems were able to filter and analyze communications even more easily, since most of the Internet's physical network was still based in the United States, through which most of Europe's communications with Asia, Oceania, Africa and South America transited. The data packets transmitted as "datagrams", the name given to Louis Pouzin's invention, were therefore relatively easy to intercept and analyze. According to Campbell's report, the NSA (following the testimony of one of its former employees) had developed a "detective" software in 1995, used to collect Internet traffic passing through nine major Internet exchanges, controlled by two interception centers named FIX East and FIX West. Campbell also reports that the NSA was able to enter into agreements with Microsoft, Lotus and Netscape at the time to monitor the global network more effectively. This observation was made in the late 1990s, when Internet users were still sharing between USENET and the early World Wide Web. In the addenda to his subsequent report, Campbell points out that once the Internet boomed and information transfer technologies became more complex, the tasks of COMINT intelligence agencies such as the NSA became more difficult to carry out.

"Since the mid-1990s, communications espionage agencies have encountered serious difficulties in maintaining global access to communications systems. These difficulties will increase from the year 2000 onwards. The main reason for this is the shift in telecommunications to high-capacity fiber optic networks. Physical access to the cables is necessary for interception. Unless the fiber network is placed within or passes

---

3 *United Kingdom-United States Communications Intelligence Agreement*, often abbreviated to UKUSA. Signed on March 5, 1946, between the United Kingdom, the United States and joined by Canada, Australia and New Zealand, establishing a collective framework for intercepting communications (COMINT) and collecting information.

through a collaborating country, effective interception is only possible if the optoelectronic transponders (once installed) are monitored. This condition is sufficient to render foreign terrestrial high-capacity fiber optic networks inaccessible" [CAM 07, p. 111].

4.3.2. *"Rendering Big Brother obsolete"*

The task of government intelligence and electronic surveillance agencies is also greatly complicated by the advances in civil cryptography, which are linked to the growing privacy concerns and the development of an Internet payment system that became a global trading platform in the 1990s. As early as 1985, Chaum suggested the principle of an anonymized transaction system based on the "blind signature" principle [CHA 85, p. 1,030], which allows a message to be authenticated without having to reveal its contents. In this particular scheme, the signature applicant conceals his or her message in a virtual envelope and the signatory receives this envelope, which he or she can sign using a private key, without having to open the envelope and reveal the contents of the message. Chaum's model was in line with his earlier work on the possibility of ensuring anonymity on the Internet [CHA 81b, p. 85]. It laid the foundations for anonymous transactions and electronic wallets and currencies. The title of his communication to the Association for Computing Machinery in 1985 was very explicit: "Rendering Big Brother obsolete". Chaum's research led him to found Digicash Inc. in 1990, which offered the first online cryptographic payment services. The technological foundations for the development of cryptographic currencies were installed, such as the famous Bitcoin, and governments and intelligence agencies began to take a serious interest in the development of civil cryptography on the Internet. The "cryptographic war" was also about to intensify, with the development of the Pretty Good Privacy (PGP) e-mail encryption program in 1991, by computer scientist Philip R. Zimmerman. PGP offered the possibility of signing, encrypting and decrypting e-mails, files, directories and databases. The message is encrypted using an encryption algorithm and a symmetrical encryption key. Each of these keys can only be used once. The message and its key are sent to the recipient so that they can decrypt the message using the private key they possess.

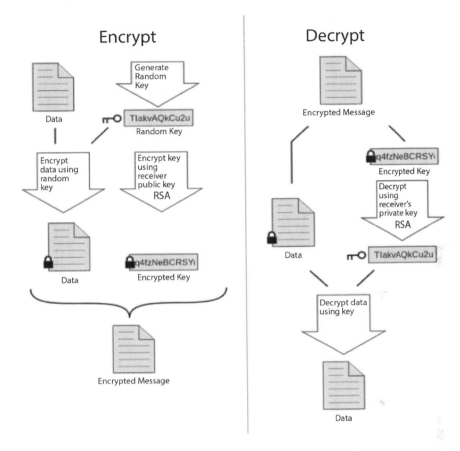

Figure 4.4. *The operating principle of Pretty Good Privacy*

Phil Zimmerman decided to freely distribute the PGP source code, which led to a long conflict with the U.S. government. The battle had to be both commercial and judicial. Accusing Zimmerman of having used his algorithm in his program without their authorization, RSA Security, founded by Rivest, Shamir and Adleman, offered the U.S. Customs Administration the opportunity to investigate the Zimmerman case. He was accused of violating the Arms Control Act of 1976, which prohibits exporting technology or equipment that could be exploited by foreign countries without the authorization of the U.S. government. The PGP source code had already crossed borders at that time and cryptography was still considered a military technique. The debate on the status of civil cryptography could begin. Faced with the impossibility of charging Zimmerman on the pretext that he had facilitated the distribution of a technology that was clearly already adopted by the general public, the U.S. government dropped the charges against Zimmerman and he was able to found his own company, PGP Inc. In 2011, together with Mike Janke, Jon Callas and Vincent Moscaritolo, he founded Silent Circle, a Geneva-based company whose core business is the development of new encryption products for Skype e-mail and communications derived from the PGP program. In a groundbreaking article from 2005, the Foundation for Information Policy Research, a British think tank studying the interactions between information technology, government and business policies and civil society, proudly titled "The 'crypto wars' are finally over – and we've won!"[4].

> "Cryptographic wars began in the 1970s, when the U.S. government began to treat cryptographic algorithms and software as ammunition and interfered with academic research in the field of cryptography. In the early 1990s, the Clinton administration attempted to force the industry to adopt the Clipper chip[5] (...). After failing, they tried to introduce the "escrow key" – a policy requiring every encryption system to hand over a decryption key to a "trusted third party", who could hand the key over to the FBI on request. They tried to break products that did not contain an "escrow key". When software developer Phil Zimmerman developed PGP, a public encryption tool for e-mails and files, the U.S. government went so far as to indict him because people had exported his product out of the U.S. without authorization. (...) However, cryptography had become a technology whose commercial use spread rapidly over the Internet – and the new industry was profoundly opposed to any bureaucracy that would prevent innovation and impose unnecessary costs. (...) In 1998, the Foundation for Information Policy Research was established by cryptographers, lawyers, academics and civil liberties advocates, with the support of industrialists, and they participated in the digital freedom campaign. (...) Phil Zimmerman, a member of the FIPR Council, who played a crucial role in the development of

---

4. "The Crypto Wars Are Over!", FIPR, available at: http://www.fipr.org/press/050525crypto.html, May 25, 2005.
5 Electronic component enabling authorities to bypass encryption if necessary in order to access information.

PGP and was also instrumental in winning the cryptographic war, said: "It is gratifying to see the last remnants of the UK cryptographic wars extinguish and I am delighted with our victory. Now we need to focus on the other threats to privacy in the post-9/11 world"[6].

The "cryptographic war" has in fact never really ceased. On the contrary, the U.S. government's inability to prevent Phil Zimmerman's PGP program from being broadcast, David Chaum's[7] launch of Digicash and Whitfield's work in asymmetric cryptography have paved the way for cyber-money and darknets. The Edward Snowden case in 2013 highlighted the efforts of intelligence agencies trying to maintain surveillance capabilities that could easily bypass the barriers created by publicly available cryptographic protocols and software. Edward Snowden's revelations came at a time when the general public had already been partly mobilized by the various scandals caused by the publication of confidential documents on the Wikileaks website, notably founded by Julian Assange. By April 2011, Wikileaks had posted thousands of pages of documents from 2002 to 2008 on its website, detailing the conditions of imprisonment of 765 Guantanamo prisoners (out of a total of 779, according to Wikileaks[8]). Prior to that, the video "Collateral murder" had revealed to the general public the conditions of the American army's terrible smear in Iraq, which had caused the death on July 12, 2007 of twelve people, including journalist Reuters Namir Noor-Elden and a 9-year-old child. On February 28, 2012, millions of documents published online revealed that Strategic Forecasting was spying on environmental activists in Bhopal, India, as well as on activists from Occupy Wall Street and PETA, an animal rights organization, all on behalf of the NSA. Among all these revelations, it was Edward Snowden's revelations that had the greatest impact and one of the major consequences of the scandal, which led the ex-employee of the American intelligence agency to seek refuge in Vladimir Putin's Russia, significantly increasing the use of anonymous online browsers, such as the now-famous Tor browser (The Onion Router).

---

6. "The Crypto Wars Are Over!", FIPR, available at: http://www.fipr.org/press/050525crypto. html, May 25, 2005.
7 Whose article published in 1981 is considered by specialists to have laid the foundations of anonymous communication networks on the Internet, D. Chaum: "Untraceable electronic mail, return addresses, and digital pseudonyms", Communications of the ACM, vol. 24, no. 2, 1981.
8 https://wikileaks.org/gitmo/.

In the summer following Edward Snowden's staggering revelations in June 2013, Tor's network saw the number of daily users quadruple from an estimated 500,000 to more than 1.5 million users per day. Today, TorMetrics charts show almost 2.5 million users per day.

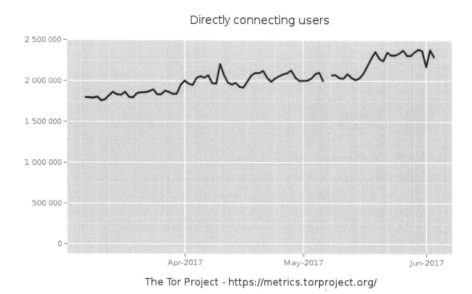

Figure 4.5. *Growth in the number of Tor users between April 2017 and June 2017*

4.3.3. *Cryptography at the service of hidden networks*

In October 2013, the Washington Post [GEL 13] revealed that the Tor Browser Bundle had been downloaded no less than 40 million times and that, in the documents updated by Snowden, there were several reports very precisely explaining how, since 2007, the NSA had attempted to set up various decryption tools to solve what the agency had called "The Tor problem". In 2007, NSA leaders met with Roger Dingledine, one of the founders of Tor and the Tor Project, an organization developing the Tor project. At the end of the meeting, the memo released by Snowden showed that the NSA was trying to find a way to de-anonymize Tor users... which was initially unsuccessful: "We will never be able to de-anonymize all Tor users at the same time. (...) Using manual scanning, we can de-anonymize a small fraction of Tor users" [BAL 13]. No expense was spared: in 2013, out of a total budget of 10 billion dollars, the NSA spent 34.3 million to decrypt services such as Tor[9].

The Electronic Frontier Foundation, which actively supports the Tor project and the online anonymity campaign, was soon to react to Snowden's revelations. On January 3, 2014, the organization produced a declaration on its website that reads as follows:

> "We thought we had won this battle. In the 1990s, EFF led the fight to protect users' rights of benefitting from a secure and efficient encryption. In collaboration with leading academics, industrialists and industry associations around the world, we have defeated U.S. President Clinton and his "Clipper Chip" [10] project. (...) According to a leak revealed by the New York Times, a project known as BULLRUN (...) is the NSA's latest attempt to bypass our democratic system and sabotage our security in complete secrecy. A lot of details about BULLRUN remain to be revealed, but we already know enough to be angry"[11].

In September 2013, the New York Times and the Guardian jointly revealed the existence of the BULLRUN program, to which the United States and the United Kingdom had allocated 250 million dollars in order to make encrypted Internet traffic accessible for surveillance by their respective intelligence agencies. However, the BULLRUN program apparently did not deploy a solution that would enable the massive decryption of networks such as Tor. While it is now possible to reveal the identity of a Tor user, it still involves significant technical resources, for a result that is not 100% reliable. In 2014, the U.S. company Cisco Netflow announced that it had found a way to de-anonymize the Tor network on a wide scale, but Tor Project developers simultaneously announced that they had fixed the loophole. In fact, since the Snowden case, the status quo regarding Tor seems to have not changed: the NSA and GCHQ, like other major COMINT intelligence agencies, are quite capable of de-anonymizing one or more Tor users using different techniques,

---

9 Peter Sayer, IDG News Service, December 9, 2014.

10 Aimed at requiring manufacturers to install a chip on personal computers that would record all user data and whose content should be available to the FBI if necessary.

11 "The Crypto Wars: Governments working to undermine encryption", Electronic Frontier Foundation, www.eff.org.

but for the time being, making Tor traffic accessible on a large scale is apparently still impossible. In addition, accessing traffic from other networks such as Freenet and I2P is just as complicated and even more difficult. However, the threat becomes clearer as far as Tor is concerned, all the more so as it is the most popular network with the public. A 2013 study already showed that 80% of users could be deanonymized by attacking Tor relays for a period of 6 months. But cryptographers are already working hard to design an effective response to this eventuality. Bryan Ford, researcher at the Swiss Federal Institute of Technology in Lausanne, certifies that "the problem is to move on to post-Tor. We've come to the point where we know that more security is possible, but there's still a lot of development work to be done" [POR 16].

This work will undoubtedly provide new techniques of online anonymity that will register with the logic of multiple technological solutions, produced in this field from the moment the first phase of the "cryptographic wars" was won and allowed this technology to spread to a wider audience. In a completely different context than today's context, the creation of the first networks has helped build a new digital culture through the development of peer to peer, a new digital culture that foreshadowed the growth of darknets. This technical evolution, which began at the beginning of the 21st Century, is also a revolution of usages and mindsets, an underground revolution with lasting consequences. The first *net sneakers* preceded the appearance of darknets. As the literature of time shows, the economic, geopolitical and security implications of their development was not yet anticipated at the beginning of the 21st Century.

5

From Sneaker Nets[1] to Darknets

The development of network encryption on the Internet is based on both an old libertarian dream and a very concrete survey, acquired during the 2000s with the development of download applications and various ways to circumvent the law in order to exchange cultural content. This type of practice was the first source of concern for public authorities and states, and is the origin of the term "darknets", whose predecessors would be the "sneaker nets" studied by Peter Biddle, Paul England, Marcus Peinado and Bryan Willman in 2003.

5.1. Peer to peer: the first darknets

According to the definition given by Stephanos Androutsellis and Diomidis Spinellis of the University of Athens, "peer-to-peer" (P2P) refers to a computer network model that is similar to the client–server model, but in which each client also acts as a server. A P2P network can be centralized (in this case connections are made through a central server) or decentralized (in this case connections can be made directly P2P, or use different connection nodes before connecting one user to another). The P2P technique is, together with the use of encryption algorithms, another essential component of alternative networks such as Tor, Freenet and I2P. P2P development, in a context where illegal downloading was identified as an increasingly important commercial threat, played a key role in the

---

1 "To sneak" means "to steal". The sneaker nets, an expression which is owed to Peter Biddle, Paul England, Marcus Peinado and Bryan Willman, inventors of the term "darknets" in 2003, refers to a "network of thieves".

emergence of the darknets' computer model, both technically and through the practices of Internet users. In 2004, the two researchers at the University of Athens described a rapidly growing phenomenon:

> "A new wave of peer-to-peer architectures is the foundation for computer distribution models such as Gnutella (2003), Seti@Home (2003), OceanStore (2000) and many others. This type of architecture is typically characterized by the sharing of computer resources (processor, cycles, storage, content) without the need to go through a central server" [AND 04, pp. 335–336].

At the time, the authors noted that this new computer model allowed large-scale data exchange within a system characterized by its "resistance to censorship and centralized control" [AND 04, p. 336]. This observation is of great importance because it underlines a twofold characteristic: the capacity for large-scale exchange between multiple users and resistance to attempts at censorship, which is at the root of the new culture that we saw emerging among Internet users at the dawn of the 21st Century, deeply linked to a radical and massive transformation of digital usage through the appearance of P2P. The philosopher Michel Bauwens even sees in it the outline of a global cooperative economy system: "The peer-to-peer revolution elicits that production emanates from civil society. Citizens contribute to common goods and the economy is created around them"[2]. The essayist seems to be delving a little into utopia, but the use of the term "common good" is crucial here, because it is at the center of the ideology that is gradually being forged around P2P, as this type of consumption of digital goods spreads, and governments and the private sector try to limit it. As early as 1996, the work of Phil Zimmerman and the Electronic Frontier Foundation showed that the American state could not oppose the dissemination of pretty good privacy (PGP); ten years later, the community of P2P technology users reacted to attempts made to block the use of new applications, the number of which had multiplied. And while in the United States and Europe, the cultural industry initially seemed to triumph in legal terms, technological responses underlined the relative powerlessness of regulatory authorities and States to contain the phenomenon. Users of P2P technologies, like Michel Bauwens, raised the notion of "common good" in order to justify the possibility of sharing products of the music and film industry through new sharing

---

2 Michel Bauwens, interview by Frédérique Roussel, *Libération*, March 20, 2015.

technologies made available to the general public, whose use seems difficult, even impossible, to limit. Worse still, in a country as large as India, ISPs readily make it easier for subscribers to connect to BitTorrent P2P file exchange platforms. The argument invoked to justify this policy is commercial and especially takes a national reality into account: access to trading platforms and VOD is a lot harder than in the West. Netflix and its VOD have only recently become established in the digital and multimedia landscape of the world's largest democracy, while Google Play Music and Spotify platforms are still absent. Illegal downloading in India is not only practiced on a massive scale, in a country of 1,266,883,598 inhabitants[3], but it is also a means of disseminating India's music and film production, which is still very abundant. By facilitating agreements with P2P platforms locally, ISPs facilitate access to a huge market of P2P operators who are as much payers as they are open sources, free from transit points that are not monopolized by millions of users seeking films and music on server-based platforms abroad, and promote the dynamism of the music and film industry by entering into agreements with broadcasting platforms in India. The model proves to be fully functional and therefore integrates local operators and providers of access and P2P in the Indian cultural and economic scheme quite effectively.

5.1.1. *P2P against the entertainment industry: David versus Goliath*

In Europe and the United States, the evolution of the relationship between P2P operators, the cultural industry and public authorities followed a very different logic. When Shawn Fanning, John Fanning and Sean Parker launched Napster's P2P file-sharing service in June 1999, the three young entrepreneurs did not know that they were launching a new digital revolution.

> "[Fanning] worked frantically, because he was certain that someone else would have the same idea, and that from one day to the next, a software company, a media conglomerate would unveil a version of the same application and Fanning's big idea would no longer be his own. And he believed it because his idea was simple: a program that would allow computer users to exchange one file for another directly, without having to go

3 CIA World Factbook, estimate July 2016, accessed June 6, 2017.

through a centralized server or an intermediary. He had heard people complaining how hard it was to find music on the Internet (...). But Fanning understood that if he combined a music search feature with a file-sharing system and, to facilitate communication, instant messaging, he could bypass the mouse trap of legal and technical complications that kept good music out of everyone's reach on the World Wide Web. (...) Almost everyone he had talked to about this idea thought it would not work. All of his more experienced buddies sneered on messaging and chat rooms online, claiming that it's a selfish world and no one wants to share. Fanning, a teenager at the time, who was still struggling to express himself, could not make himself clearly understood. He argued that people would do it because... well, just because. What he had in mind was that this program could unleash the true potential of the web and viral growth of the online community, the transgressive power of the Internet would break through barriers and transform our preconceived ideas about business and cultural content. He simply could not put it in words in order to convince his fellow programmers that his idea would change the world. Whether you like it or not, that's what Napster did: change the world" [GRE 00].

Shawn Fanning's contribution to building a new model of the digital economy and new uses of the Internet was essential. After the RSA algorithm and the PGP program, Napster's creation 18 years ago on June 1, 1999, represented a major turning point and a decisive contribution to the emergence of darknets. In 1999, Napster revealed the shocking arrival of an exchange protocol that allowed cultural content to be exchanged outside the classical music industry, but also the start of an online community that will never cease to develop, carrying the idea expressed by John Perry Barlow in 1996 with his "Declaration of the Independence of Cyberspace". A pioneer of P2P exchange services, Napster, as Time reported in 2000, "forced record sales companies to rethink their business model and music industry, and artist advocates to defend intellectual property. It forced content providers like Time Warner, Time's parent company, to wonder what content would even be in the near future" [GRE 00]. In doing so, and in the eyes of millions of Internet users, Napster has represented the digital version of David and Goliath's myth.

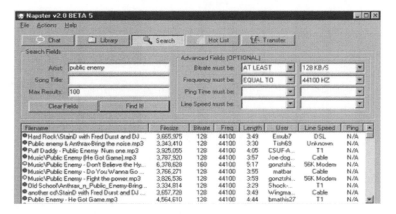

Figure 5.1. *Napster software in 1999*

Napster's activity quickly caught the attention of the Recording Industry Association of America (RIAA). The RIAA, whose acronym is despised by a large part of the Internet community, filed a complaint on December 2, 1999 against the service created by Shawn Fanning. After two years of legal proceedings, the Napster service was closed down in 2001 for infringement of copyright law. Nevertheless, the damage had been done, and the damage is irreparable for the cultural industry, given that Napster permanently implemented the simple idea that if the new information and communication technologies now not only make it possible to communicate, but also to exchange files online, then there is no reason why multinationals and States should be able to oppose it. In a way, Napster shined a spotlight, to a considerably broad audience, on the arguments that had been defended by Phil Zimmerman and the EFF during the battle over PGP. The Napster case has, on the one hand, partly radicalized the opposition between a community of users and, on the other hand, major digital players and states.

Figure 5.2. *Shawn Fanning (left) and Sean Parker (right), co-founders of Napster (Photo Wikipedia)*

The Napster case ended in 2001, but the confrontation between supporters of free P2P exchange and the cultural industry was only just beginning. This new battle, which somehow followed the cryptographic war of the late 1990s, was to determine the true origin of darknets. The term was used for the first time in the particular context of post-Napster by Biddle, England, Peinado and Willman, when the main problem identified by governments and Internet regulators was the illegal exchange of files. Successive attempts to develop a legal arsenal that would make it possible to suppress this type of use, and the technological replicas that were systematically triggered by these attempts, have made it possible to constantly shape and improve the technology that serves as the bedrock of darknets today. After Napster, it was Gnutella, then eMule, Kazaa and Soulseek who took over the same principle, but with increasingly greater bandwidth capacity, which allowed P2P to pose a threat to the film industry as well, while films began to be exchanged massively over the Internet.

Figure 5.3. *In order, the logos of eDonkey, eMule, Gnutella and Soulseek. For a color version of this figure, see www.iste.co.uk/gayard/darknet.zip*

Napster had popularized a new cultural practice of file exchange, but its technical specifications made it a relatively centralized and vulnerable system, as its rapid closure had demonstrated. Those which followed, or were jointly developed, were already moving much more toward decentralized solutions based on user networks and communication nodes for data transfer. This was already the case with eDonkey2000, a multisource file transfer protocol that appeared in 2000 and was then closed in 2006, again because of the lawsuit launched by RIAA. This is even more evident with the more famous site, eMule, launched in 2002 and employed the Kad protocol, created by Petar Maymounkov and David Mazières, a true parallel network defining its own communication nodes in a completely decentralized structure. Gnutella, developed by Justin Frankel and Tom Pepper of Nullsoft, adopted the same decentralized architecture that made this type of P2P network relatively unstable, but also relatively difficult to neutralize.

Simultaneously, P2P services maintaining a centralized or semicentralized architecture had also begun to offer their services following Napster. This was the case of Soulseek, which combined chatrooms (forums) and P2P clients, a bit like Napster, but also of another famous site, Kazaa, developed by Sharman Networks and the Estonian programmer Jaan Tallinn. Introduced on the market (in a free and premium paid version) in March 2001, Kazaa quickly became the subject of numerous lawsuits in the Netherlands, the United States and Australia, which eventually not only led to a ban on downloading the software in Australia, but also resulted in convictions of many Kazaa users around the world. In Duluth, Minnesota, Jammie Thomas-Rasset, a 30-year-old single mother, was ordered to pay $9,250 to six music industry majors: Sony BMG, Arista Records LLC, Interscope Records, UMG Recording Inc., Capitol Records Inc. and Warner Bros. Records Inc., for downloading 1,702 songs via its Kazaa account. The proliferation of such cases gradually helped to raise the Internet community and public opinion against institutions such as RIAA and music industry giants, accused of attacking users by demanding exorbitant compensations for the use of new technologies that these same companies had not been able to foresee and were now trying to neutralize by terrorizing their users. Only a few years after the fall of Napster, David had already grown up in the face of Goliath.

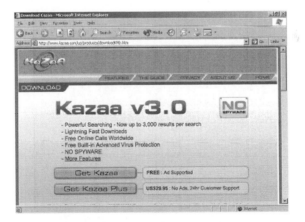

Figure 5.4. *Kazaa customer exchange window*

5.1.2. The BitTorrent revolution

If the download war followed the cryptography war, then the issue of encryption and encryption of exchanges would soon return to the heart of strategies for circumventing legislation, which was also toughening up in France with regard to illegal downloading, with the creation of the *Haute Autorité pour la diffusion des œuvres et la protection des droits sur Internet* (HADOPI) in 2009. Nevertheless, if Napster and Kazaa P2P services could be countered and could even, in Kazaa's case, expose their users to lawsuits, then the architecture of Gnutella and Kad/eMule would already foreshadow the concept of darknets that Tor, Freenet and I2P designers would later popularize.

Another P2P exchange protocol, however, would consolidate the network architecture model that systems such as Tor, Freenet and I2P now benefit from: the BitTorrent protocol, on which an American programmer, Brad Cohen, started working in 2001. At a time when Napster was kneeling to the courts, Brad Cohen was preparing for a second revolution that would once again transform the practices and uses of the Internet in a sustainable manner, while ironically, the digital economy was experiencing its first serious crisis that same year with the collapse of the NASDAQ stock market. In 2001, many believed that the ephemeral odyssey of the Internet was about to end. In fact, it was just the beginning.

Brad Cohen is not California-born like Shawn Fanning, but is originally from New York City, where he was born in 1975, making him five years older than the Napster creator. His father taught him the basics of programming when he was only six years old. After two years at the State University of New York in Buffalo, he dropped out of school in 1995 and entered the booming start-up business environment in 1995. He entered MojoNation, a company developing a service to fragment confidential files into different encrypted parts and redistribute them on a network of computers connected to each other. If a person needed to download the fragmented and encrypted file, he or she could do so from multiple sources simultaneously, which Cohen found to be a distinct advantage over the Napster- and Kazaa-type system, where the source remained unique, which, in addition to causing vulnerability and confidentiality problems, could unduly lengthen the download time in the case of a very large file. Downloading different parts of a file divided between several sources could significantly reduce download time.

It was from this model that Cohen designed the BitTorrent protocol, which was allowed to download a file from several sources quickly and simultaneously. In the system designed by Cohen, the file downloaded by a user is itself shared again, or rather "hashed" on the network between several users who, by sharing the fragmented file, ensure the improvement of its distribution. Thus, in a BitTorrent type system, we call a user who downloads a file a "dryer" and a user who shares it a "seeder"; but as more users download the same file, the number of "seeders" logically increases, which increases the download speed of the file.

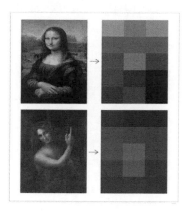

Figure 5.5. *The principle of hash function in pictures (source: Wikipedia). For a color version of this figure, see www.iste.co.uk/gayard/darknet.zip*

An educational example of the principle of hash functions applied to images: here we consider a hash function consisting of converting a high-resolution image into a very low-resolution print.

The print is much smaller in terms of memory. It loses much of the information, but it remains sufficient to quickly distinguish two images.

In April 2001, Cohen left MojoNation in order to devote himself to the development of BitTorrent, programmed in Python. In 2004, Cohen founded his company, BitTorrent Inc. with his brother Ross Cohen and partner Ashwin Navin. As soon as the BitTorrent protocol was made available on the network, it became so popular that it generated considerable traffic worldwide. In 2004, a study showed that P2P traffic accounted for 62% of global Internet traffic[4] and that BitTorrent alone accounted for 53% of P2P traffic, representing one-third of global Internet traffic with some regional variations: 16% of European traffic, 33% of American traffic and 65% of

4 https://torrentfreak.com/bittorrent-the-one-third-of-all-internet-traffic-myth/.

traffic in Asia. In 2005, the share of P2P in world traffic rose to 71%. The share of the global bandwidth mobilized by BitTorrent fell to 21%, which did not mean that Brad Cohen's protocol was less successful, but simply that other downloading solutions persisted and even multiplied in a very short time to offer Internet users a considerable offer of illegal downloads. BitTorrent still faced competition from eDonkey, which used 35% of the bandwidth in the United States (slightly more than BitTorrent, which used 30% of the bandwidth) and 50% in China (equal share to BitTorrent). With the closure of eDonkey in 2006, the decline of eMule and the disappearance of Kazaa, BitTorrent took the lion's share of the P2P universe in the following years, which accounted for 80% of world traffic in 2007 [LIE 07, p. 2]. BitTorrent therefore quickly found itself under fire from criticism and attacks.

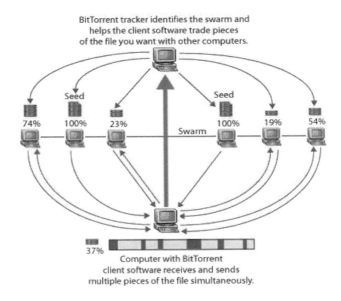

Figure 5.6. *The working principle of the BitTorrent protocol (BitTorrent.org). For a color version of this figure, see www.iste.co.uk/gayard/darknet.zip*

Many lawsuits have resulted in the closure of multiple sites using the BitTorrent protocol to offer illegal downloading solutions, including Supernova.org, Torrentspy, Lokitorrent, Demonoid and Mininova. This time, however, the legal counterattack does not make it possible to fight against trafficking and practices that are developing massively on equal terms. Some sites, including the famous Pirate Bay, who self-proclaim to be "the galaxy's most resilient BitTorrent site", make it their specialty and glory to close their site and reopen it a few days later, from servers hosted in a different country each time.

Figure 5.7. *The Pirate Bay homepage*

5.1.3. *The emergence of darknets*

Parallel to the success of BitTorrent, as governments try to tighten up the regulation of the phenomenon, P2P is truly entering the era of closed networks of encrypted exchanges, with downloading software offering users access to password-protected communities and P2P forums in order to ensure the confidentiality of exchanges. These communities, which can use the BitTorrent protocol or operate on the principle of closed circuits, such as Waste and selective forums, like newsgroup models such as DC++, form just as many parallel networks as Microsoft engineers already described in 2003, calling them darknets. Indeed, recalling the definition suggested by Peter Biddle, Paul England, Marcus Peinado and Bryan Willman, darknets were "a collection of networks and technologies used to share digital content" [BID 03], such as P2P networks, private newsgroups and encrypted messaging. At the time, Microsoft's four engineers established that although copying audio and video content was an ancient practice, it was limited to a non-economic model until the appearance of P2P. From the moment it appeared, it became a reprehensible model for Napster, eMule and Kazaa, but was still "easily controllable and easy to neutralize by the authorities". Yet, the authors recognized that the "development of packet switch networks and advancements in codec[5] technology had made it possible to illegally make high-quality content available at lower cost", whether virtually with P2P or physically with CD-burning software (such as Nero Burning ROM). For the four authors of this landmark article, between the 1990s and the 2000s, we went from "bubble-networks" and "sneaker net" networks, in which the "duplication of works was organized between groups of friends by audio K7 or floppy disks containing computer programs via K7 recorders and computers", to the model of interconnected networks of exchanges such as Gnutella and Napster, which were the first darknets for Biddle, England, Peinado and Willman. The democratization of the Internet from the late 1990s onwards made these darknets, sneaker nets and bubble-networks "accessible to a large number of users, who could now be connected by and between a centralized service". Although the first attempts were still unsuccessful because of the still too centralized (Napster) or slow evolutionary (Gnutella) character of these networks, Biddle, England, Peinado and Willman predicted a rich future for the darknet from the first matrix of illegal downloading: "We see no obstacle to the darknet becoming more and more efficient". This efficiency also concerned the economic plan, given that in another study in 2007, Eric Johnson, Dan McGuire and Nicholas D. Willey, employed at the Tuck School of Business' Center for Digital Strategies, noted that legal downloading had increased by 163.3% from 2004 to 2005 giving a total of 366.9 million downloads, representing $363.3 million, which was still far from the $10.52 billion generated by the CD industry, but today in 2017, we can see what has happened to the CD, compared to the commercial fate of mp3 [JOH 07, p. 7].

However, another problematic aspect of illegal downloading is pointed out by researchers of the Tuck School: "Because of the aggressive legal tactics used by the cultural industry against individuals, the next evolution of P2P will aim to protect and conceal P2P users even more effectively. These changes are likely to create more security concerns. These three types of defences are anonymization, trusted networks and redistributed downloading" [JOH 07, p. 18], in other words, Tor-type encrypted networks, private networks and the redistribution of encrypted BitTorrent files. Four years apart, Biddle, England, Peinado and Willman for Microsoft and

---

5 Encoding and decoding technique for digital streams, especially audio and video streams.

Johnson, McGuire and Willey for the Tuck School identified two solutions for the future of P2P darknets: I2P and Freenet.

> "Many new customers offer different forms of encryption to conceal the identity and transfers of their users. (...) Today, the most advanced of these clients uses multiple layers of encryption to conceal the identity of users. The I2P (Invisible Internet Protocol) network is used thanks to a modified version of the Gnutella client, called I2Phex. The network hides both the identity of the sender and the recipient, by only identifying users with "cryptographic routing keys" [JOH 07, p. 19].

Four years earlier, Biddle, England, Peinato and Willman saw Freenet as the future of illegal downloading and darknets, and emphasized the strong ideological component that underlay the creation of this genuine alternative network. According to them, the P2P philosophy assumed that a significant proportion of users adhere to the postcapitalist concept of sacrificing one's own resources for the common good. With a 56K modem, allocating part of the bandwidth to resource sharing was a substantial sacrifice. If platforms like Gnutella were diverted from this collaborative philosophy, another approach was to make it mandatory, as in the case of Freenet. Freenet users were forced to allocate some disk space for the entire network [BID 03, p. 3].

The evolution of sneaker nets that became darknets toward a new model of true parallel networks was already impending in 2000, when Shawn Fanning, who was in the midst of judicial turmoil at the time, answered Time Magazine's questions. During the interview, Fanning admitted to having kept an eye on his remarks in public, and even his clothing, in order to give as little credit as possible to the arguments of his opponents' lawyers. He thus acknowledged that he was no longer able to wear a T-shirt that had been sent fraternally by the group of hackers Cult of the Dead Cow, the creators of one of the very first encrypted navigation tools, destined to be used on a large scale: Peekabooty, developed in 2001. From that moment on, Time journalist Karl Taro Greenfeld summed up the ideological stakes of the confrontation at the beginning of the 21st Century in a few words: "Since the trial started, Napster has been wrapped up in what I would call a siege mentality, an 'us against them' attitude, directed against the record labels and the press that have forced Fanning to retreat deeper into his shell" [GRE 00].

The portrayal is happy and effectively describes the temptation represented today by darknets that Biddle, England, Peinato and Willman already called "small-worlds" in 2003: finding refuge in a community, protected by encryption of unwanted intrusions and coercion of laws and authorities. In 2017, we are no longer at the dawn of P2P, and the emergence of parallel networks has consequences that are today linked far more closely to security issues, in the eyes of public authorities.

5.2. "Netopias" and darknets: the appearance of parallel networks

"The combination of strong and unbreakable public key cryptography with virtual communities in cyberspace will produce interesting and profound changes in the nature of economic and social systems. Crypto-anarchy is the cyberspace realization of anarchic-capitalism, transcending national boundaries and liberating individuals to enable them to achieve the economic arrangements they desire in a consensual way. Serious cryptography, as exemplified by RSA (Public Key Algorithm) and PGP (Pretty Good Privacy), provides encryption that cannot be broken even with all the computing power of the universe. This guarantees security and privacy. Public key cryptography can rightly be considered a revolution" [MAY 94].

5.2.1. Cypherpunks and cyberpunk

Timothy C. May can be considered a major figure in the "cypherpunk" or "cryptoanarchist" movement in the 1990s. This former engineer and chief scientist of the Intel company who retired in 2003, has made himself known, alongside his technical discoveries, particularly in the field of alpha particles, by making a notable contribution to cryptoanarchist ideology at the dawn of the 21st Century. With the *Crypto Anarchist Manifesto*, published in 1992, and then the *Cyphernomicon* in 1994, May defines in a detailed and radical way, the political project of the "netopias" that flourished on the network in full development from the late 1990s to the early 2000s, as sneaker nets, hackers and darknets were also developing by taking advantage of the innovative movement that seized the computing domain. Four years before John Perry Barlow published his "Declaration of the Independence of Cyberspace", May gave birth to the cypherpunk movement with his *Crypto Anarchist Manifesto*, released in 1992. The term "cypherpunk" itself was created by Jude Milhon, a U.S. civil rights activist from the 1960s and pioneer computer scientist, with a play on words between "cypher", which means "encrypt", the term "punk", ("good-for-nothing" or acrostic: "People Under No King") and the term "cyberpunk", a movement initiated by science-fiction writer William Gibson in the 1980s. The first cypherpunk band was formed in the early 1990s around the figures of John Gilmore, Eric Hughes, Timothy May and Judith Milhon. All four computer scientists were convinced that the joint development of cryptography and the Internet could change the socioeconomic organization of the world in the long term, and even call the pre-eminent role of governments into question. The cypherpunks organized focus groups in both physical and virtual reality, which were conducted from the mailing list majordomo@toad.com and the toad.com site, created by John Gilmore on August 18, 1987, making it one of the first .com domains in the network's history. Gilmore himself was a former employee of Sun Microsystems and the founder of Cygnus Support. As a committed libertarian activist, Gilmore was also a key contributor to the development of the GNU project, the open source operating system developed by Richard Stallman in 1983, and a co-founder of the Electronic Frontier Foundation. Eric Hughes is an American mathematician and programmer, author of *A Cypherpunk's Manifesto* in 1993. In June 1993, Hughes appeared masked, along with Gilmore and May, on the cover of *Wired*, which was dedicated to the cypherpunk movement.

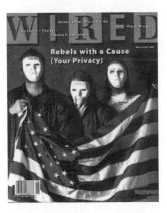

Figure 5.8. *Cover of the May/June 1993 edition of* Wired. *The three masked figures are Eric Hughes, John Gilmore and Tim May*

The cypherpunk movement clearly assumed to be a filiation with the cyberpunk wave, embodied by William Gibson and Bruce Sterling from the 1980s onwards. William Gibson, born May 17, 1948 in Conway, South Carolina, is an American science fiction writer and one of the leaders of the cyberpunk movement. Cyberpunk (an association of the words "cybernetic" and "punk") is a subgenre of science fiction related to dystopia and hard science fiction (that is to say, SF based on hypotheses and realistic and detailed scientific content). It presents a near future, with an advanced society in the fields of information technology and cybernetics. It was in the Washington Post on December 30, 1984, that an article by Dozois entitled "SF in the Eighties" described William Gibson's work, and more specifically his novel *Neuromancer* (1984), as "cyberpunk". He also described a whole group of "weird" young authors who wrote in the Cheap Truth fanzine: Bruce Sterling, William Gibson, Lewis Shiner, Pat Cadigan and Greg Bear. The cyberpunk "movement" was thus born. *Neuromancer* is William Gibson's first science fiction novel. Published in 1984, it is generally considered to be the founding novel of the cyberpunk movement that has inspired many works such as the manga *Ghost in the Shell*, and *Akira* and *The Matrix* in cinema. It is the initiation of a genre that some have described as "naturalistic science fiction", an exercise in anticipation, based on the development of contemporary technologies.

"I feel that the best use of science fiction today is to explore contemporary reality, instead of trying to predict the future... The best thing to do with science today is to use it to explore the present. Earth is today's alien planet"[6].

At the dawn of the 21st Century, the Internet seems to offer the dematerialized realization of the visible fantasy in Gibson's ultra-realistic science fiction. In *Neuromancer* (1984) and *Engraved on Chrome* (1986), Gibson describes a world transformed by the use of computers and cybernetics, dominated by powerful multinationals and split through its virtual counterpart, the "Matrix", the cyberspace paradise of hackers. Although Gibson's work belongs to the so-called "genre" of literature, it has nonetheless had a great influence in computing and engineering circles, gained by the pioneering spirit associated with the development of the Internet. In 1993, in the Los Angeles Times, Laurence Chollet [CHO 93] spoke of William Gibson's "second view", whereas Laura Evenson spoke of

6 Excerpt from an interview given to CNN on August 26, 1997.

the "oracle of cyberspace" in the San Francisco Chronicle of September 24, 1996. For a whole generation that lived through the democratization of computer tools, Gibson had painted the colors of a technological dystopia, to which the cypherpunks would try to give not just a reality... but a virtual reality.

In fact, the vindicated crypto-anarchists such as Tim May do not doubt that the development of new technologies could profoundly modify the relationship between the individual, the community and the State, in the sense of a new kind of social pact, sealed by public dissemination of the cryptographic techniques applied to communications on the Internet.

> "We cannot expect governments, corporations and other major organizations to facelessly grant us privacy by act of benevolence. It is to their advantage to talk about us, and we should expect them to do so. To try to stop them is to fight against the realities of intelligence. Intelligence doesn't just want to be free, it wants freedom. Intelligence tends to fill up the available storage space. Intelligence is the youngest, strongest cousin of Rumor; Intelligence has a lighter foot, has more eyes, knows more, and thinks less than Rumor. (...) We, the Cypherpunks, are dedicated to building anonymous systems. We defend our privacy with cryptography, anonymous return systems, digital signatures, and electronic money" [HUG 93].

The electronic money Hughes is talking about already existed in 1993. Mathematician and cryptographer David Chaum developed *ecash* in 1983 [CHA 81a] then Digicash in 1990, two cryptographic electronic money systems. As for Hughes' other ambitions, it seems that in 1993, technology could keep its promises. In 1992, Tim May already anticipated the development of encrypted networks, the emergence of which would mark the next decade, in his Crypto Anarchist Manifesto. Here are a few excerpts:

> "A spectrum haunts the modern world, the spectrum of crypto anarchy. Computer technology is about to provide individuals and communities with the opportunity to communicate and interact with each other in a totally anonymous manner. (...) The technology for this revolution – and it will surely be both a social and economic revolution – has theoretically emerged in the last decade. (...) Attention has so far been focused on

academic conferences in Europe and the United States, which are closely monitored by the National Security Agency. But it is only recently that computer networks and personal computers have had sufficient speed to make this idea a reality. And the next decade will bring enough speed to make it economically feasible and unstoppable".

5.2.2. Crypto-anarchism and activism: Peekabooty

In this instance, the decade that followed saw the development of P2P systems, and decentralized architectures and protocols such as BitTorrent[7]. The innovations introduced by Shawn Fanning and Brad Cohen paved the way for the emergence of true parallel communication and exchange networks, to which four Microsoft engineers gave the name darknet in 2003 [BID 03]. Other innovations will soon emerge, taking advantage of the loophole opened by the creators of Napster and BitTorrent, as governments and authorities attempt to curb illegal downloading by amending legislation and adopting new coercive measures. This context, combined with advances and research in the organization of computer networks and encryption, allows us to move to a new phase by designing true alternative networks that literally superimpose themselves on the Internet and allow you to browse and exchange files in (almost) anonymous ways. The best-known of these networks is Tor, developed in the late 1990s under the aegis of the U.S. government, and on which this book focuses. Nevertheless, Tor's success has somewhat eclipsed other similar systems, of which we will say a few words. These are mainly Peekabooty, Zeronet, Telecomix, Steemit, Diaspora, Syndie, Freenet and I2P.

Peekabooty was created by the hacker group Cult of the Dead Cow, founded in 1984, whose T-shirt Shawn Fanning was delighted to have received, but was regrettably not able to wear because of his legal troubles[8]. Peekabooty, which no longer exists today, remains an extremely interesting founding project in the history of darknets, since it was developed independently and exclusively in order to provide dissidents of authoritarian regimes and inhabitants of countries dominated by dictatorial governments with the possibility of anonymous access to the Internet, bypassing the filters

---

7 See section 5.1.1. P2P against the entertainment industry: David versus Goliath.

8 See section 5.1.2. The BitTorrent revolution.

set up by the authorities to control Internet access. The principle of this system, which is again based on public key cryptography, is to offer authoritarian nationals the possibility of passing through relays located outside the monitored and controlled area in order to be able to surf the Internet and download data.

Figure 5.9. *Cult of the Dead Cow homepage*

The installation of Peekabooty was intended to allow Western users to allocate personal space on their computers in order to serve as relays and thus facilitate the existence of Chinese, Saudi and other authoritarian countries' citizens. A first demonstration of Peekabooty was held at the DefCon show in Las Vegas in July 2001 and another at CodeCon 2002 in California. As Lee Dembart reported at the time, for the International Herald Tribune, Peekabooty benefited greatly from the advances made possible by software developments in the field of downloading:

"In a way, it looks like the decentralized network that exists within Kazaa and Morpheus, the popular music sharing software that followed in Napster's footsteps. But instead of exchanging files, Peekabooty simply has to transfer web pages on the fly. Nothing is stored. In addition, the network must allow completely anonymous navigation. Everything will be encrypted to prevent eavesdropping, but encryption has not yet been installed, so security cannot be guaranteed" [DEM 02].

In retrospect, we can see that the journalist of the Herald Tribune did not yet fully understand Kazaa and Morpheus' function, which were not exactly decentralized systems. As Antonin Billet and Karine Solovieff noted for 01Net, Peekabooty is closer to Gnutella and Freenet.

Figure 5.10. *The Peekabooty Beta version interface shows a user (center) connected to a normal user, a second one behind a Firewall (with tape on its mouth) and a third one using NAT (Network Address Translation) protocol that allows it to bypass blocking attempts*

5.2.3. *Freenet*

Despite an initial phase during which Paul Baranowski, creator of Peekabooty, was pleased to count 35,000 downloads of the software in two weeks, the project perished due to lack of funds and development. However, this was not the case for Freenet, which had a happier destiny and has survived to this day. Established at Edinburgh University in 1999 by Ian Clarke, who did not have much academic support, Freenet was rapidly put under an open source license and its development was supported by Sourceforge and made available online [CLA 99]. Freenet is a P2P network of interconnected nodes. Each node has its own storage space, the datastore, which it makes available in read/write for the other nodes. It contains the addresses of the nodes to which it is connected, as well as the keys to decipher the data. The datastore is divided into two parts of equal size: the cache and the storage. The cache stores the keys it sees transiting through. The storage stores the keys closest to it. When the datastore becomes too large, keys that have not been used for a long time are deleted. The more nodes in the network, the more storage space there is and the faster the addressing and transfers.

> "We can describe Freenet as an adaptive peer-to-peer network application that allows publication, copying and retrieval of data while protecting the anonymity of users and viewers. Freenet operates as a network of identical nodes that pool their storage space in order to house data files and cooperate to direct requests to the nearest storage point. No centralized search or indexing protocols are used. The files are labeled independently of their location and dynamically copied to the storage spaces close to the applicant, and deleted where they are not needed. It is impossible to find out the origin or destination of a file circulating through the network, and it is difficult for a connection node operator to determine the physical content of the relay and be held responsible for it" [CLA 00, pp. 46–66].

Traditional network systems, analyzed by Ian Clarke and his colleagues in 2000, store data on one or more fixed addresses, creating a point of vulnerability. Freenet therefore offers data storage that is decentralized, fragmented and dynamic. This dematerialized storage system, in the words of its developers, "does not seek to guarantee anonymity for the general use of the network, only with regard to data transfers" [CLA 00, p. 2]. However, there are two connection modes: darknet mode and openet mode. In darknet mode, you can manually enter trustworthy nodes to create your interconnections. In openet mode, one node connects without preference to the others. The darknet mode is preferable for anonymity, but requires knowledge of trusted node IDs (friends).

In 2000, Freenet's designers distinguished several other attempts, more or less similar or related to Freenet, such as the MixMaster Remailer, based on the Mixnet scheme described by David Chaum in 1981 [CHA 81b, pp. 84–88], Goldschag, Reed and Syverson's onion routing work [GOL 99, pp. 39–41], and the Freedom system[9]; however, all of these systems did not offer a

---

9 Zero-Knowledge Systems, http://www.zks.net/2000.

satisfactory dematerialized and secure storage solution, according to Clark and his colleagues. Instead, Freenet's designers mentioned Anonymiser[10], Crowds [REI 99, pp. 32–38], Berthold and Federrath's WebMIXes system [BER 01], Rewebber, Publius, a censor-resistant online publishing system, Goldberg and Wagner's Temporary Autonomous Zone (TAZ) system, and even archiving systems and protocols such as Eternity, distributed.net, India, Intermemory, Akamai and, the best-known, Free Haven.

It is therefore clear that at a time when Freenet's developers were publishing the results of their work, some five years after the main cypherpunks and crypto-anarchists manifestos were released, an international community of researchers, computer scientists and cryptographers were working diligently to go beyond the model presented with Napster by Shawn Fanning. With Freenet, Clarke and his team believed they had come up with the ideal solution, combining asymmetric cryptography and dematerialized storage. Although the complexity of Freenet still restricts its use on a large scale, with Ian Clarke modestly admitting to accommodating just under 30,000 daily users in 2011, the project has managed to survive and improve up to now, which is not the case for most of the experiments mentioned above. Since then, however, many other initiatives have been launched, such as Retroshare, Zeronet and I2P, to cite a few examples.

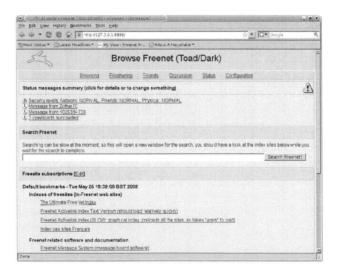

Figure 5.11. *Freenet's interface*

---

10 http://www.anonymiser.com.

5.2.4. It is a small world...

Another type of encrypted communication software called Retroshare, developed in 2006 and regularly improved and updated since then, is halfway in between a P2P system and an encrypted network. The open-source application provides file sharing, e-mail and instant messaging, online chat, Skype-based instant video and audio communications, forums and friend-to-friend networking. A little like how Freenet presents in its darknet mode, once connected to Retroshare, the user generates a pair of encrypted keys that are used to connect the user to the friends he or she accepts and with whom he or she allows encrypted exchanges.

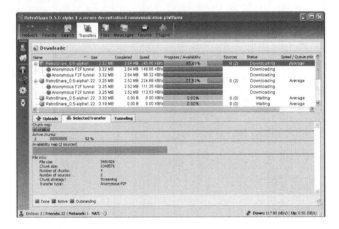

Figure 5.12. *Retroshare download interface (01. net)*

In January 2014 on Twitter, Retroshare developers announced that they hosted up to 5,800 users per day.

Figure 5.13. *Twitter account of the Retroshare team*

As for Zeronet, it was developed very recently in Hungary by a community of computer scientists gathered on the Reddit forum, who published the first version on January 12, 2015. It is an online sharing and communication platform, based on the BitTorrent protocol and on the principle of asymmetric cryptography, since the user also receives two keys, one public and one private, when he connects. Lastly, Zeronet also uses the blockchain system used by electronic currencies such as Bitcoin, which registers, emits and validates transactions through the computers that keep up the network. This validation is a calculation in the resolution of which any person can participate, by presenting the help of his processor and a part of his computing capacity. Once a transaction is validated, each computer that has participated in its validation is allocated a certain amount of electronic money, proportional to its participation in the calculation. In the case of Zeronet, this collaborative computing system contributes to the functioning and stability of the network. When logged in, the Zeronet user has access to a platform supporting a true independent network, on which he can navigate using a dedicated search engine, but where the hosted sites cannot yet exceed the size of 10 MB. Just like Retroshare, Zeronet is compatible with Tor and I2P networks.

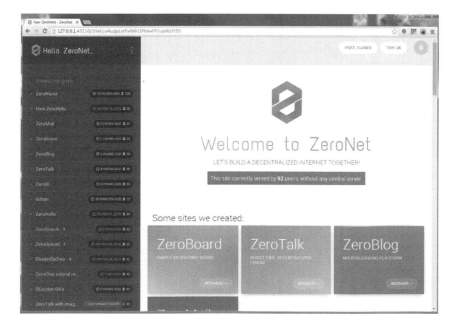

Figure 5.14. *Zeronet homepage*

Diaspora does not exactly fall into the category of darknets because it is a social network, but it nevertheless offers a type of service that comes close to it since, true to its slogan "The only social universe in which you are in control", Diaspora offers to join a network in which each user hosts on his own computer and acts as a server for his own relay connection (called pod) and his own information. The developers of Diaspora (which was launched in 2010) therefore ensure that under this principle and contrary to Facebook, no recovery of personal data for commercial purposes can be carried out since the user is the only one to host the data that is put online on the social network (personal information, videos, photos, text, etc.). It was designed by Ilya Zhitomirskiy, Dan Grippi, Max Salzberg and Raphael Sofaer, four MIT students who raised over $200,000 from donations for their project. Among the generous donors was a certain Mark Zuckerberg, who was very interested in this social networking project developing privacy as the main business argument. Today, Diaspora has one million subscribers.

In 1999, Clarke and his colleagues asked an interesting question: "Is Freenet a small world?" According to mathematicians Duncan J. Watts and Steven H. Strogatz [WAT 98, pp. 440–442], small-world networks or "microwave networks" are particular and extremely tight types of networks, in the form of grid connectors with particular properties, which guarantee efficient information transfer. In this type of network, interconnection means that you are only five or six intermediaries away from a known or friendly person. By extension, these "micro-worlds" become genuine digital utopias – "netopias" – protected from the outside world, but developing enough interactions and interconnections to constitute autonomous entities, superimposed on the network in the case of darknets. While Freenet is a relatively modest model of small world, the development of alternative networks over the past 20 years has given Freenet and other projects a genuine "regional specialization" in digital environment, as Watts and Strogatz put it.

Another example of a "small world", finding refuge in the "hidden Internet", I2P is also a true parallel network, created in February 2003. This was initially a suggested modification for Freenet, which developed as a competing network in April 2003, metamorphosing into I2P in July of the same year.

Figure 5.15. *I2P*

I2P is a project whose goal is to build, deploy, and maintain a network providing secure and anonymous communications. People using I2P have control over the trade-off between anonymity, reliability, bandwidth usage and latency. In this network, there is no center that could be pressured to compromise the integrity, security or anonymity of the system. The network integrates its own dynamic reconfiguration in response to various attacks, and has been designed to use new resources as they become available. Of course, all aspects of the network are public and available free of charge.

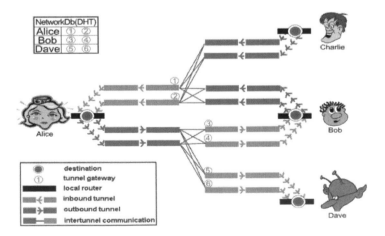

Figure 5.16. *Tunnel principle in I2P. For a color version of this figure, see www.iste.co.uk/gayard/darknet.zip*

At first glance, the network consists of a pile of nodes ("routers") with a number of virtual inbound and outbound unidirectional paths (called "tunnels"). Each router is identified by the cryptographic identifier "RouterIdentity". Client applications have their own cryptographic identifier ("Destination") that allows them to send and receive messages. These clients can connect to any router and allow temporary allocation (lease) of a few tunnels that will be used for sending and receiving over the network.

In Figure 5.16, Alice, Bob, Charlie and Dave all have their routers, with only one local destination. They each have a pair of incoming tunnels with two jumps per destination (identified as 1, 2, 3, 4, 5 and 6). When Alice and Bob talk, Alice sends a message to one of her outgoing tunnels (in pink) with the target of one of Bob's incoming tunnels (3 or 4, in green), causing the client application to query the network database, which is constantly updated.

To deal with a wide range of attacks, I2P is fully decentralized and consequently, there is no directory server with performance and reliability statistics. Each router is responsible for selecting peers appropriate to the anonymity, performance and reliability needs of users. The network uses a significant number of cryptographic techniques and algorithms. Contents sent over I2P are encrypted through three layers of onion encryption (used to verify message reception by the recipient), through tunnel encryption (all messages passing through a tunnel are encrypted by the tunnel gateway to the tunnel exit point), and through the encryption of data between routers.

The increase in darknet networks, of which we have just given a few examples, seems to actualize Tim May's ideal, described in the *Crypto Anarchist Manifesto*, or to even give reality to the project depicted by Hakim Bey [BEY 91] in his work *TAZ*, published in 1991, that is to say the creation of spaces of moving freedom, appearing and disappearing in such a way as to escape any institutional control. The various software solutions in favor of online anonymization and participation in a real network superimposed on the Internet may suggest that not only a new type of digital usage, but also a new type of business model is being developed here. However, while many promoters of the darknet networks identify with this libertarian ideal, it must be acknowledged that the reality of the phenomenon offers a landscape far removed from this primary utopia.

None of these networks can currently compete with the Tor network in terms of popularity, which in a few years has become the "dark star" of darknets because of consequent media coverage. This reputation, which has led to the Tor network's growing popularity, raises the more serious question of the economic viability of darknets as innovative digital tools. It also raises other questions related to the rather paradoxical history of Tor's creation, which interestingly enough, distinguishes itself from its darknet "cousins", while appearing today as *the* supreme darknet.

5.3. The Tor network

"There is only one time when it is essential to awaken. That time is now, We cannot wait till somebody wakes you. You are the crazy ones, the misfit, the rebel, the troublemaker, the one who see things differently. We are not fond of rules and have no respect for statuesque, you can imprison us and oppress us we don't care we are legion. Only thing you can't do is ignore us because we change things. We create revolution's, we empower a free society in the here and now. And while they are afraid of us with their cronyism and kleptocracy, their bureaucracy and ideology, their police and spies calling us criminals, we see creation. Because the people who are crazy enough to think they can change the world, are the ones who do"[11].

This manifesto is published on the Tor network by the administrator(s) of the Digital Gangster site, a site that provides visitors with full open access to a wide range of information and instructions in order to take advantage of operating flaws in various applications and software. Available at the address "digigangxiehugqk.onion"[12], the Digital Gangster site offers simple text files to transmit its tips and tricks to those who want it, as well as other rather surprising information. This includes telephone numbers, e-mail addresses, personal addresses, and posting units of 3,000 soldiers and Venezuelan army employees. In a similar manner, the site also offers a long list of e-mails, phone numbers and names of about 100 FBI employees.

---

11 The full manifesto is available in Appendix 2. That kind of manifesto is not rare and is greatly inspired by the "hacker manifesto" written on January 8, 1986 by Loyd Blankenship (also known as "The Mentor") after his arrest.

12 This address will be obsolete by the time you read this book.

Figure 5.17. *Digital Gangster homepage*

The owner of the site also posts instructions online to exploit a flaw in the Allio Applicant Portal software, which allows you to put interfaces online for registering inscriptions and applications from students, professors and assistants in a portion of American universities and a number of institutions in other countries. When the Allio Applicant Portal went online, as detailed by the hacker, it had a loophole (at least until May 31, 2017) allowing SQL injection, in other words the possibility for a hacker to exploit this loophole in order to hack into or even modify the Allio Applicant Portal database. With a certain irony, the author of the post points out that he tried to contact the software manufacturers first before making the flaw public on the Tor network:

Disclosure Timeline:
* Contacted vendor via email (no response) – 17/03/2017
* Called their call center (confused employees)
* Called their corporate offices (more confused employees)
* Emailed a supposed security contact there (no response) – 28/04/2017
* Disclosed vulnerability – 31/05/2017
# Digital Gangster [2017-05-31]

Box 5.1. *Chronology of the launch of the Allio Applicant Portal operating fault*

This means that between March 17 and May 13, whoever discovered and published the flaw tried to contact the sales department, the call center, the head office and a so-called "security contact" by e-mail and telephone without success, before distributing this information freely to the entire Tor network.

This type of site is exemplary of some of the content published on the Tor network. According to the black legend that is now being echoed in the media, this darknet, whose popularity continues to grow, is home to a wealth of pages and sites promoting perfectly illegal activities such as child pornography, arms sales and the drug trade, which are abundantly available on the Tor network. The .onion Hidden Wiki address directory gives a fairly accurate idea of the type of content hosted by Tor and its deliberation is, in itself, edifying.

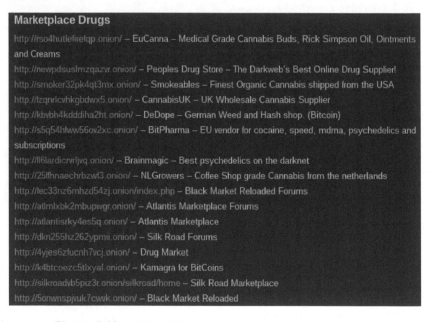

Figure 5.18. *Hidden Wiki type address directory screenshot*

5.3.1. *The origins of Tor*

The online encyclopedia Wikipedia defines Tor today as a global, superimposed and decentralized computer network, consisting of a number of servers that function as relays for a network that allows anonymizing connections. Tor also designates a browser that allows you to surf the Internet without leaving a trace, based on Firefox: Tor Browser, also developed by the Tor Project, a Massachusetts-based non-profit organization founded by Roger Dingledine and Nick Mathewsone in December 2006. This organization is supported by the Electronic Frontier Foundation, an international non-profit organization based in San Francisco whose stated goal is to defend individual rights and access to new technologies, in what it considers to be cases of abusive interference by states and multinationals in the digital domain. The support for the Tor project follows the policy advocated by EFF very logically, one of whose historical founders is John Perry Barlow, the author of the "Declaration of Independence of Cyberspace". Grateful Dead's former lyricist is a major figure in the movement, which has been called "crypto-anarchism" and "cyber-free", bringing together members of the Internet community: computer scientists, intellectuals, cryptographers and activists, fighting to have the Internet recognized as a zone independent of the power of governments and international and multinational institutions. Three years ago, Barlow conducted a question-and-answer session for users on the Reddit forum for a few hours, during which an Internet user asked the following question: "How do you think cryptography will evolve in the face of privacy issues?" He gave an answer that sums up the philosophy stated quite well today by EFF leaders, like those of the Tor project: "I think we need to strike a balance between the visibility of the individual and that of the institution. Right now, things are going in the wrong direction. People are electronically exposed. While the NSA and others are draped in impenetrability. It cannot work. And our first answer is encryption, the second is that we tear off their veil and the third is that we use our differences to make them impotent. Everyone is stranger than they imagine" [BAR 13].

Tor was originally born out of a collaborative project between the U.S. Naval Research Laboratory and the NGO Free Haven Project. The "onion routing" principle was developed in the mid-1990s by mathematician Paul Syverson and computer scientists Michael G. Reed and David Goldschlag, in order to develop an encrypted communication system for the benefit of the U.S. military and intelligence services. Therefore, the primary purpose of "onion routing" was not to protect the anonymity and privacy of ordinary users, but to allow military intelligence personnel and employees to work in complete secrecy online. "As military communications assets become increasingly dependent on civilian infrastructure, it is important to be able to use this infrastructure, while simultaneously protecting against traffic analysis. It would also be useful to communicate anonymously, especially during intelligence-gathering activities in public databases" [SYV 14]. At a time when Internet traffic was exploding in the late 1990s and the World Wide Web was becoming a means of communication, it was not conceivable for a CIA or other intelligence agency employee to connect, particularly on foreign soil, to the Internet site of the institution using it and thus risk being exposed. Onion routing was one of the solutions found to deal with this new situation and to answer the question asked by Michael Reed, one of the first designers of the operating principle behind the Tor system:

> "The use was intended for the Department of Defense and Intelligence (collection of data in public access, coverage of the means and human resources deployed, and so on...). It was not about helping dissidents of authoritarian regimes. Not to assist criminals in covering their electronic footprint. Not to help BitTorrent users avoid MPAA and RIAA lawsuits. Not to give a 10-year-old kid the means to bypass a pornography filter. Of course, we knew that these hijacked uses would be unavoidable, but it was of no real importance in relation to the problem we had to solve (and if these usages gave us better traffic coverage to conceal the use we wanted to make of the network, it was all the better... As I once told a senior officer, to his greatest disarray"[13].

In 2002, two new recruits joined the project development team being overseen by the Naval Research Laboratory: Roger Dingledine and Nick Mathewson, two MIT engineers employed under contract by DARPA and the U.S. Naval Research Laboratory's Center for High Assurance Computer Systems. Over the next few years, the new team was to work on the development of a new onion routing system that would eventually give rise to Tor. It was from there that Tor's strange paradox took shape, which was initially financed by the U.S. government. Roger Dingledine, whose CV states that he even worked for the NSA for a month, also quickly realized that designing an online anonymization system that would only be used by military or intelligence agency personnel did not make much sense, as he stated in 2004: "The U.S. government simply cannot develop an anonymization system for everyone and reserve the use of it. Because every time a connection is established with this system, we'll say: 'Oh, here's

13 Quoted by Yasha Levine, [SYV 97].

another CIA agent', if they are the only ones using this network"[14]. As Pando's journalist Yasha Levine reported, Paul Syverson made the same observation in January 2014: "If you have a system that solely depends on the Navy, everything that comes out of it will clearly be linked to the Navy. You need a network that supports traffic open to other people" [LAW 14].

5.3.2. *The Tor paradox*

Did the U.S. Naval Research Laboratory draw a logical premature conclusion from the finding that Dingledine had already made in 2004? The fact remains that in the same year, the U.S. Navy cut funding for the Tor project and that it was released as a free license and recovered by the Electronic Frontier Foundation, an organization co-founded by the very libertarian John Perry Barlow. From the austere military environment, Tor passed into the hands of crypto-anarchists and Internet rights defenders. The history of Tor's genesis could not become more paradoxical: from a military project, Tor became the spearhead of the fight for the right to anonymity on the Internet. Was it so surprising? By becoming a tool accessible to the general public, Tor was fulfilling Reed's ambition: to become a traffic anonymization system that would make it possible to conceal activities from government, military or intelligence agency employees, who would use it and conceal their activities more effectively by hiding in the crowd. It does not matter, as acknowledged by Reed in 1997 to one of his superiors, who would benefit from Tor's services in the future and why....

The government has not stopped funding the Tor project, even after the withdrawal of the U.S. Navy. The Pando Website reveals that among the multiple financial backers of the Tor project are Google, the Swedish government, the EFF, the Pentagon, the United States Department of Defense and even the International Broadcasting Bureau, created after Bill Clinton's promulgation of the International Broadcasting Act in 1994, and dependent on the Broadcasting Board of Governors, which oversaw the financing of non-military international broadcasting structures. So here we are at the heart of the Tor Project paradox, a non-profit organization managing the development of the Tor network and the browser of the same name, supported by EFF, but still largely by the U.S. government. And while

---

14 Roger Dingledine, "Wizard of OS", conference given in Berlin on June 11, 2004, quoted by Yasha Levine, [SYV 97].

intelligence agencies and authorities are concerned about the criminal activities that may be taking place on the Tor network, in addition to anonymization activists welcoming the development of the network, the same intelligence agencies commend themselves on the fact that the network is gaining important and increasingly effective coverage of activities that require a communication channel, that is both highly frequented and anonymous. The authorities' attitude toward Tor would in this case be somewhat schizophrenic, as well as that of the EFF, whose former director, Shari Steele, has taken over the leadership of the Tor project and intends to turn it into a tool for the general public, as explained by the online magazine The Kernel, which reports that Shari Steele has challenged the U.S. Department of Justice, the NSA and the FBI, after having served as a member of the U.S. Department of Justice. Again, it is no less paradoxical to see this tireless digital rights activist at the head of the Tor Project, which is still largely funded by the U.S. government. And she herself easily acknowledges the major disadvantage of this financial dependence on the institutions to which she has so often been led to oppose: "It is not ideal. These are government contracts. (...) I come from the EFF, where we haven't received a single penny from any government. There was a red line. But this one doesn't exist in Tor"[15]. Similarly, Shari Steele has had to defend himself against the numerous accusations against the Tor network, which is suspected of being far more permeable to security breaches and intrusions by the NSA than its designers suggest, as they claim that each of the identified breaches actually strengthens the network's security. Lastly, it seems that the NSA has been able to partially de-anonymize the Tor network, but the strengthening of encryption protocols and the increase in traffic make it difficult to deanonymize the entire network. Tor experienced an explosion in traffic during the summer of 2013 following Edward Snowden's revelations and it now counts between two and 2.5 million users every day. Nevertheless, the vast majority of Tor users have never visited a hidden Website, as this service accounts for only 3–6% of Tor's total traffic. Simply browsing the Internet anonymously is a service that is immensely more popular than browsing or exchanging data over the encrypted network to which Tor gives access, particularly since, although installing and using Tor does not require specific technical skills, browsing the Tor network may

---

15 Reported by Seth Rosenblath, "New Tor director Shari Steele gears up for challenging future", *The Parallax*, December 30, 2015, available at: https://www.the-parallax.com/2015/12/30/new-tor-director-shari-steele-gears-up-for-challenging-future-qa/.

appear to require more solid technical skills and represent a significant, albeit poorly identified, risk.

5.3.3. *How Tor works*

Tor's operation is based on a decentralized architecture, similar to that of Freenet or I2P and uses onion routing, like the latter. A query on the Tor Browser Bundle browser (and its associated search engine DuckDuckGo) will pass through three "relays", in other words Tor project collaborators and/or users whose computers host data on the Tor network. The term "onion routing", which gives Tor its name (The Onion Router), refers to the encryption technique of data transiting over the network through relays, each of which adds a new layer of encryption to the signal it transmits [CHE 17, p. 27]. When browsing with Tor, a series of intermediate connection nodes are used to reach any site – whether on the web surface or Tor's darknet – to decrypt and re-encrypt the data at each relay, as if a group of people were passing a message from hand to hand in a series of envelopes and each member of the group were removing an envelope, before sending it back to Tor. Only the final server will be able to access the information conveyed to deliver it, while protecting the identity of the sender.

These types of systems work with PGP pairs of keys, based on the model conceived by RSA designers and Phil Zimmerman, that is to say an asymmetric cryptography form. The service will select a relay to be used as an entry point into the Tor network. The hidden service then delivers its public key to the introductory relay and creates a descriptor file, containing its public key and the name of its introductory point. The hidden service will then sign the descriptor file created by the relay with its private key (on the blind signature model described above); this will generate a .onion address that will be publicly distributed and disseminated on the clear web, in order to allow a user to find the hidden service. The .onion address is a 16-character hash of the hidden service's public key. At this level, the distributed hash table plays the same role as the Domain Name System (DNS) does for the clear web. Where the DNS assigns a more memorable name to an IP address, the DHT turns the public key into a .onion address. Once a user is aware of the .onion address of the private service, he or she can use the Tor Browser to enter this address in the Tor Browser bar to create a relay circuit consisting of a relay randomly selected by Tor, and at least three other relays, through which the user's request and the relay that served as an introductory point for the user who wished to retrieve a hidden service, will pass. The message to be sent by the user will therefore contain (1) the address of the relay taken at random by the user, (2) the address of the relay which served as an introduction point to the hidden service that the user wants to reach and (3) a one-time secret password (created using an algorithm) and the communication is encrypted because of the public key used by the hidden service (from which the .onion address was generated). When the user has made a request through the Tor network, the hidden service recipient will receive and decrypt this message using their private key to find out the address of the relay point and the one-time password. It will then send a meeting message, containing the one-time password at the user-defined relay meeting point. This relay then alerts the user that the connection has been established. The communication between the user and the hidden service takes place through the relay meeting point, but also through three randomly selected relays on each side. This communication is encrypted from beginning to end. As the TorProject.org[16] Website points out, by using a fairly efficient image that blends the imagination of both *Bullit* and the *Petit Poucet*, using Tor is like leaving foot traces while pursuing a chaser, while simultaneously being able to erase the traces, given that each relay borrowed can only really identify the nearest one and it is therefore – *a priori* – impossible to trace the circuit (from a compromised relay) constituted by the three relays, used on either side by the user and the hidden service.

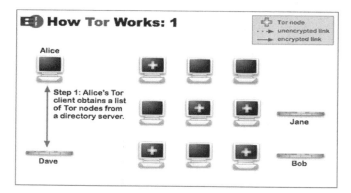

Figure 5.19. *Alice, a Tor user, gets a list of hidden services through an address directory. She can connect to a node/relay to contact one of these hidden services (Torproject.org)*

16 https://www.torproject.org/about/overview.html.en.

The circuit is composed of all the relays used to establish the communication (at least three). In the circuit, each relay only knows the relay to which it transfers encrypted data. It is therefore impossible to know the entire route by hacking into a relay.

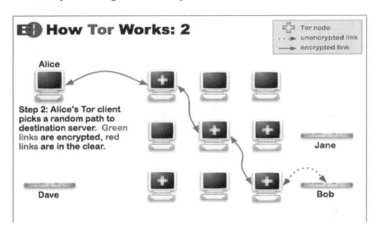

Figure 5.20. *Alice chooses a random relay to connect to a hidden service. The green indicates encrypted links and the red indicates the clear ones. For a color version of this figure, see www.iste.co.uk/gayard/darknet.zip*

For added security, the circuitry used for communications between the user and the required service changes every 10 minutes to further complicate the task of tracing it.

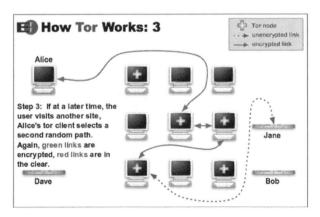

Figure 5.21. *If Alice visits another site or connects to the same site after 10 minutes, a new circuit with new relays will have been established. For a color version of this figure, see www.iste.co.uk/gayard/darknet.zip*

5.3.4. *The principle of the .onion address*

A .onion address has 16 characters, all of which are digits between two and seven and lower case letters. These addresses are generated by Tor from a public key. An example is given by the Facebook version of Tor at facebookcorewwwi.onion.

Figure 5.22. *There is a Facebook on the Tor network, officially managed by Mark Zuckerberg's company*

The Facebook address on the Tor network is noticeably easier to remember than most .onion addresses, such as this one: http://yjuwkcxlgo7f7o6s.onion/ (address to the Tor project archives).

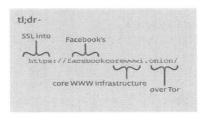

Figure 5.23. *Facebook address on Tor (facebook.com)*

To obtain this result, it is possible to modify the .onion address by using a software named Shallot, which allows you to assign a clearer and more easily memorable meaning to part of the address. In terms of the private key used by a hidden service, Shallot will determine a character sequence that can be partially modified. Beyond sixteen characters, the site specifies that the calculating time for a standard computer is a few billion years, giving a fairly accurate idea of the computing power required to crack a private key. Shallot simply offers the ability to determine a part of the address yourself, rather than calculate it using the key.

The example first shows how effective Tor encryption technology is. Flaws do exist, of course, and have consequently been exploited by the NSA and other monitoring agencies, but the developers and designers of the Tor Project take advantage of them each time in order to learn some lessons from the experience and strengthen the robustness of the system. Furthermore, the ability to "customize" addresses allows some services to continue guaranteeing their users the benefit of anonymity and encrypted data exchange, while ensuring greater visibility on the network, unlike the majority of hidden services using an address that can only be found through address directories such as the Hidden Wiki. The main problem for Tor users is finding hidden sites whose addresses are, for the vast majority, impossible to remember. Hidden Wiki is the name given to a hidden Wikipedia service that can only be accessed using the Tor browser. The address of the Hidden Wiki(s) is a .onion address. They thus lead to real directories listing the existing services on the Tor network, in a more or less exhaustive and accurate way, by trying to classify and categorize them. The first thing that a Tor user who wants to browse the .onion sites' networks will have to do is to search, on the clear web or from the Tor Browser Bundle search engine, for the address of a valid and correctly updated Hidden Wiki. Although the operation presented some difficulties until a few years ago, it is now extremely easy and a simple search on a classic search engine will already yield satisfactory results. The Hidden Wiki is, or rather "was", a .onion Website. In fact, the service is now widely accessible on the clear web. A glance at the search results obtained easily shows this, as the first result you get is the address https://thehiddenwiki.org, as well as an address in .onion, in the following results, now accessible online from any traditional search engine.

If this directory, accessible online without having to go through the Tor Browser Bundle, mostly compiles perfectly functional .onion links, it is interesting to note that the bridges between the clear web and the dark web have largely developed because of the use of Web2Tor, a software that allows access to the hidden services of Tor, that is to say to the .onion sites, from a traditional browser without using the Tor Browser Bundle, or even needing to install it. It is possible to do the opposite, in other words to connect to clearnet services without having to leave the Tor network, because of Tor2Web that works in the same way, thus offering to switch from one to the other through a proxy and without the help of Tor. The .onion version of the Hidden Wiki can thus be easily accessed using Web2Tor, as shown in the screenshot in Figure 5.24.

Figure 5.24. *The Hidden Wiki via Tor2Web*

Web2Tor (and Tor2Web) is a proxy that redirects all HTTP and HTTPS feeds to a Tor client using the default port 127.0.1:9050. Using Tor2Web therefore makes .onion sites visible and accessible to users who are not connected to Tor, by replacing the .onion address with .onion.to. Tor2Web and Web2Tor were developed in 2008 by American computer scientists Aaron Swartz and Virgil Griffith. The goal of the two Tor2Web developers was to provide journalists and whistleblowers with a way to access Tor's services more easily without having to install it. Tor2Web and Web2Tor do not offer the same guarantees of anonymity as Tor itself. The software merely provides a proxy service that theoretically allows content to be published anonymously from the Tor network and made accessible on the clearnet in addition to access to the Tor network from the clearnet through an anonymized channel. However, once users switch from the Tor network to clearnet, anonymous browsing is no longer guaranteed. Aaron and Griffith's aim was essentially to facilitate the access to Tor for a wider audience, but above all to enable Tor users to make their publications more easily accessible from the clearnet. Swartz and Griffith's approach was political. In an interview with the newspaper *Wired*, Swartz explained that while the Tor network was a formidable tool for anonymous content publishing, its character, which was "not user-friendly", that is to say technical and not accessible to the general public, limited its success and audience. Swartz wanted to "produce a hybrid through which people can publish things by using Tor and making it visible to anyone on the Internet"[17].

---

17 Interview by Kim Zetter, "New Services Makes Tor Anonymized Content available to All", wired.com, December 12, 2008.

Figure 5.25. *Aaron Swartz and Virgil Griffith (Wikimedia common photos)*

Having long been limited to trial versions, Tor2Web and Web2Tor were finally distributed as stable versions from 2014 onwards and are now widely distributed and easily accessible. As the tor2web.org Website makes clear: "Tor2Web only protects content publishers and not those who consult them. As a reader, installing the Tor Browser will ensure you much better anonymity, a greater confidentiality of authentication than using Tor2Web. Tor2Web replaces security with convenience and ease of use"[18]. For those who want to look at Tor's hidden sites without installing the software, Tor2Web offers a simple solution: simply replace the .onion extension with .onion.to, .onion.city or .onion.cab, and you are done.

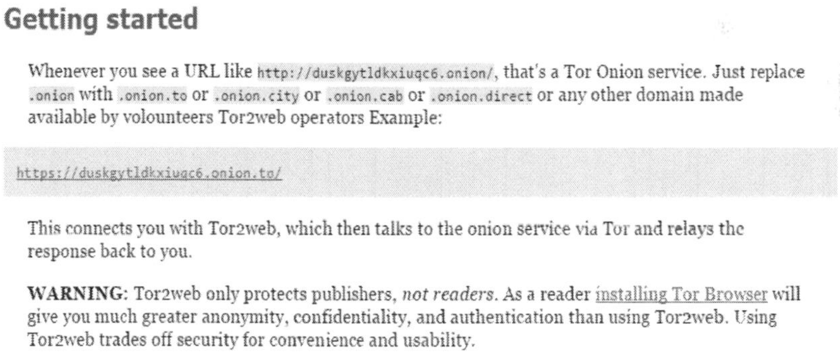

Getting started

Whenever you see a URL like `http://duskgytldkxiuqc6.onion/`, that's a Tor Onion service. Just replace `.onion` with `.onion.to` or `.onion.city` or `.onion.cab` or `.onion.direct` or any other domain made available by volunteers Tor2web operators Example:

```
https://duskgytldkxiuqc6.onion.to/
```

This connects you with Tor2web, which then talks to the onion service via Tor and relays the response back to you.

WARNING: Tor2web only protects publishers, *not readers*. As a reader installing Tor Browser will give you much greater anonymity, confidentiality, and authentication than using Tor2web. Using Tor2web trades off security for convenience and usability.

Figure 5.26. *Using Tor2Web*

There are now free search engines, accessible from the clearnet, using Tor2Web and offering any user the ability to perform a quick search on the .onion network from the Internet, as easily as using a traditional search engine

---

18 https://tor2web.org/.

to query the Internet's DNS. This is the case of onion.city, which has become onion.link, or onion.cab, ahmia.fi and of course onion.to. Some services, such as onion.direct, have had to close down because of complaints about services that provide access to illegal activities (the seriousness of which varies from illegal downloading to child pornography and the sale of narcotics online), but similar services are emerging as a substitute for them and are becoming increasingly popular. As the Naked Security Website noted on February 18, 2015: "One of the consequences of this type of operation is that Onion City search results appear as classic web pages, making them visible to you, me, the Onion City search engine and, for the first time, Google" [STO 15]. The next small digital revolution may well begin there. Tor2Web search engines now allow hidden sites to be referenced on the clear web: "At the time we're writing this, about 650,000 dark web pages have made their way through Google's index via Onion City. Of course – as any small business owner will tell you – just because Google knows a site exists does not mean that the pages of the site will be well indexed. But these pages are to some measure integrated into the mix now, taking advantage of their first glimmer in the spotlight" [STO 15].

Figure 5.27. *The Onion Cab search engine homepage*

5.3.5. *An evolution of Tor uses thanks to Tor2Web?*

Obviously, trying to connect to a hidden Tor service hosting reprehensible activities is of little interest: as is very clearly stated on the Tor2Web homepage, the use of this software and its derivatives allows you to trade anonymity for ease of use. In short, if you intend to order cocaine on one of the many sites offering this type of service, your IP address will not be hidden and you may have some problems with the authorities. On the other hand, the Tor2Web principle may perhaps represent the compromise solution that could give the darknet a new aspect, by pulling it away from the criminal environment in which it is still immersed and making Tor, in particular, its primary vocation:

"Tor's creators remain staunch defenders of the benefits of Tor. Roger Dingledine, one of the early developers, said: "There is a significant need for hidden services, when human rights defenders use them, for example, to access Facebook or to blog anonymously (...). These uses are new and have great potential" [CHE 17, p. 29].

The ability to access .onion sites via search engines such as Tor2Web and even via a simple Google search, which is now starting to index .onion pages, in a way responds to the difficult problem of cybersecurity in the face of hidden networks, summarized by George Bush's former Secretary of Homeland Security from 2005 to 2009:

"The first challenge is that there is nothing criminal about Tor's use of anonymity, but there is no clear way to distinguish criminals from innocent users if they are all anonymous. If there were no criminals using Tor, the authorities would not exert such pressure on Tor and the anonymization it offers. Unfortunately, it's very difficult to blame someone for their actions if their identity is unknown, and it's difficult to unmask a person without having the ability to de-anonymize all Tor users" [CHE 17].

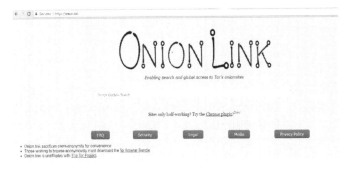

Figure 5.28. *Onion City, having become Onion Link*

Being able to benefit from Tor's services in order to publish content anonymously and being able to use Tor2Web services to view content without this anonymity adds an interesting variable to the complicated equation of online security and crime. Indeed, there is no interest in viewing child pornography images or videos using Tor2Web, nor is there any interest in buying cocaine – and even more so selling it – through this application. On the other hand, publishing sensitive and censorship-prone content gives Tor and Tor2Web its full significance and usefulness. Furthermore, for a dissident or journalist fearing censorship or repression in an authoritarian regime, wishing to conceal his identity or simply make his blog more difficult to close, publishing content on Tor is totally justified, and it will be justified all the more so if they know that a much larger audience is likely to discover their site and their stories without necessarily going through the Tor Browser, but by means of a simple search on the Internet. For example, this is typically the case of sites whose purpose is to facilitate the work of "whistleblowers" such as WikiLeaks, of which there is of course also a version on the clear web, but which nevertheless provides a good example to illustrate the present situation. In fact, there is a WikiLeaks interface that allows you to offer documents for publication only accessible on the Tor network and which, in theory, guarantees the anonymity of the depositor.

No other application provides access to the WikiLeaks interface that houses confidential or leaked documents. Any attempt to make a request on Google, Ahmia, Onion City or Onion Cab to access this type of WikiLeaks service will receive such a response.

Figure 5.29. *Attempted access to the WikiLeaks form (Tor service) document deposit using Onion Link*

However, it is quite possible for a simple user to use Onion Link (or another search engine) to consult documents published on Tor by WikiLeaks, after having been transmitted by an anonymous contributor who has used the services of Tor Browser Bundle directly for this purpose. There is absolutely nothing illegal about consulting them and no Internet user can be worried about that, whereas on the content editor's side, the Tor network provides some security and protection since it is very difficult to close this site without it reappearing on another part of the network a few days later, worrying the managers and owners of the site, whose identity remains unknown. The complicated equation proposed by the darknet in terms of cybersecurity and anonymity protection may not be solved, but the progressive referencing of .onion sites on Google Search, using Tor2Web technology, seems to be opening a doorway as it always guarantees Tor's interest in the fight against censorship, but differentiates between hidden sites promoting illegal activities and those that fall within a completely legal framework. Furthermore, the increased referencing of .onion sites may pave the way, by increasing the visibility of this new type of domain, to an extension of the Tor network's commercial value in a context where the search for anonymity is becoming an added value for a growing number of users. Although the darknet still serves as a safe haven for illegal activities, which is discussed in more detail in Chapter 6, the darknet is no longer a haven for traffickers, hired killers and child pornography enthusiasts. Recently, musician Aphex Twin released his latest album on the darknet. Facebook, as we have seen, has also invited itself onto the Tor network. We can also gradually see media and think tanks multiplying on the darknet. According to journalist and subject matter specialist Jamie Bartlett, the darknet, and initially the Tor network, which is by far the most popular darknet network, may well become much more mainstream in the years to come:

> "The Internet is going to become more interesting, more exciting, more innovative, more horrible and more destructive. This is good news if you value freedom, autonomy and democracy. This is also good news if you want to browse illegal pornography sites or buy and sell drugs with impunity. Not entirely shady, nor entirely radiant. It won't be one aspect or the other that wins, but both" [BAR 14].

Of the two Tor2Web developers, at least one will not have the opportunity to know if his software will have contributed in the coming years to popularize the Tor network to the extent of making the darknet an Internet 3.0. Aaron Hillel Swartz, who developed Tor2Web with Virgil Griffith in 2008, was arrested on January 6, 2011 by MIT Police[19] for

---

19 The police unit specifically responsible for enforcing the law – including IT – on the campus of the Massachusetts Institute of Technology.

hacking into the MIT system using a guest account that had been illegally assigned to him and downloading articles from the academic journal *JSTOR*. Swartz was charged with computer and electronic fraud, accumulating a penalty of $1 million and 35 years in prison. After refusing to plead guilty, which would likely have allowed him to spend only six months in a federal prison, Swartz was found hanged in his Brooklyn apartment in June 2013. His name has since been added to the Internet Hall of Fame. His partner Virgil Griffith continued to develop Tor2Web before announcing the release of a functional and stable version of Onion City on February 11, 2015. The development of this type of tool contributes greatly to the increase in traffic on the Tor network, which is in line with the wishes expressed both by Tor co-founder Roger Dingledine and those of the current Tor project director, Shari Steele: to make Tor a tool for the general public in the coming years. Ironically, the fulfillment of this wish is perfectly in line with the views expressed by one of the fathers of onion routing, the mathematician of the U.S. Navy, Paul Syverson, who wanted to create traffic on the encrypted network large enough to perfectly mask the activities of military personnel and intelligence agency employees who might use it. The irony here is the converging ambitions of the leaders of the EFF, the Tor Project and the military. Nevertheless, there is growing concern among the authorities about the impressive development of illegal and criminal activities on the Tor network and other darknets, in addition to cybercrime, which has become a real strategic problem for governments over the past decade, more so than just a judicial concern.

6

Geopolitics and Cybersecurity

The development of "hidden networks" over the past few years has taken place against a backdrop of increasing threats to electronic security. The phenomenon of computer piracy has taken on a new dimension since the 1990s and it is important to explain its evolution and present its prospects.

6.1. From "hacktivism" to "cyberwarfare"

On January 15, 1990, AT&T's telephone network suffered a breakdown that caused general astonishment because of its size – 60,000 households were deprived of a telephone for 9 hours – but mainly because of the cause or rather the absence of a real cause of the crash. Without being able to establish it with confidence, AT&T officials and public authorities suspected a piracy operation. The incident unveiled a new form of crime that accompanied the telecommunications revolution in the last decade of the 20th century. The authorities were quick to take the threat very seriously [STE 92]. On May 7–9 1990, a large police operation known as "Sun Devil", involving 150 officers, was conducted in 14 states on the initiative of the Secret Service and Gail Thackeray, assistant to the Attorney General of Arizona. It led to the seizure of 42 computers and 23,000 floppy disks. The operation, as announced by the U.S. government, was to "send a clear message to any computer enthusiast whose interests violated the ethical use of computers" [LEW 91]. The operation was directed against a group of hackers known as Legion of Doom, whose name was a reference to the group of super villains in the DC Comics universe. Members of the Legion of Doom, who bore the pseudonyms of Erik Bloodaxe, Lord Digital, Phiber Optik, Lex Luthor, Monster X, The Prophet, Doc Holiday, Pucked Agent

104, Dr DOS, Blue Archer and Unknown Soldier, were suspected of several crimes and in particular of piracy and damage to electronic and computer systems. Congress itself authorized the secret services to investigate this type of crime under Title 18 of Section 29 of the United States Code, which recognized the existence of "fraud with access device". The scale of the operation drew public attention and shed light on this relatively new phenomenon that was emerging with the democratization of the Internet: hacking. The slang term "hack" was created in the 1960s by students at the Massachusetts Institute of Technology in order to describe an ingenious way of solving a problem, such as cutting out the bottom of a bottle and turning it into a container, or using razor blades glued to a clothespin to strip a wire. For the students of the prestigious American institution, the "hack" could correspond to more ambitious gags, such as the one that led prankers to hook a life-size replica of a police car to the dome of the prestigious institution. As science fiction writer Bruce Sterling summed it up, as the "hack" became more technical and complex, it could provide a comforting sense of power and security, bestowed by mastering particular technical skills. "The deep attraction for this sensation of technical and elitist power should never be underestimated" [STE 99, p. 36]. The democratization of information technology and the development of the Internet have given a new meaning to hacking. Shortly after the "Sun Devil" operation, which had raised as much concern among government officials as it did among individual freedom activists who were protesting against the spectacular display of force, Harvard teacher Laurence H. Tribe already saw the urgent need to adapt U.S. law to this new context: "New technologies should lead us to a more detailed examination of what values the Constitution is precisely seeking to preserve" [LEW 91].

6.1.1. *The first hackers*

The years that followed saw the emergence of new groups of hackers, each more eager than the other to demonstrate their know-how. After the Legion of Doom, it was the Masters of Deception, Neon Knights, L0pht Heavy Industries, Cult of The Dead Cow and the Chaos Computer Club who took over in the 1990s, as well as a few isolated individuals whose exploits – or pretenses – were no less. In 1998, members of L0pht certified to Congress that they were capable of rendering the Internet inoperative within 30 min. The hacker "Mafiaboy" succeeded in neutralizing the sites of Yahoo, Amazon, eBay and CNN. His colleague "Dark Dante" hacked into the phone lines of a radio station in order to easily win a prize that was no more than a Porsche 944[1]. One of the most famous hackers of this period is undoubtedly Kevin Mitnick, known as "The Condor", who managed to hack into the databases of Pacific Bell, Fujitsu, Motorola, Nokia and Sun Microsystems and even tried – unsuccessfully – to gain access to the Pentagon. He was the first hacker on the FBI's list of 10 most wanted fugitives. Arrested in 1995, he was sentenced to 5 years in prison and published two books in 2002 and 2005: *The Art of Deception* and *The Art of Invisibility*, before becoming a consultant in computer security.

Writer Bruce Sterling summed up the libertarian and somewhat Nietzschean philosophy that guides the actions of some hackers by writing in his book, *The Hacker Crackdown: Law and Disorder on the Electronic Frontier*, the particular philosophy of a hacker under the evocative pseudonym, "Emmanuel Goldstein"[2]:

> "Technical knowledge and specialized knowledge, of any kind that can be obtained, belongs by right to individuals brave and daring enough to discover them – by any means. The devices, laws or systems that prohibit access to it, as well as the free dissemination of knowledge, are provocations that any free hacker with any respect for him or herself must fight unceasingly. The 'intimacy' of governments, corporations, and other soulless technocratic organizations must never be protected at the expense of the freedom and initiative of the individual techno-rat" [STE 92, pp. 64–65].

"What will computer crime look like ten years from now?" asked Gail Thackeray, in an interview with Bruce Sterling, "Will the situation have improved?"[3] A quarter of a century later, the development of the Internet, like that of darknets such as Tor, I2P and Freenet, has, on the contrary, offered much greater opportunities for cybercrime, which is now manifested in actions of unprecedented magnitude. Computer hacking is no longer just a matter of amateurs and groups of activists using the names of super villains and pseudonymous warriors, nor is it just a concern for the cultural industry

1 Reported by Mark Ward, "A brief history of hacking", BBC News, June 9, 2011.
2 Emmanuel Goldstein is a character from George Orwell who, in *1984*, excellently embodies the state enemy, leader of a mysterious "Brotherhood" aimed at destabilizing the Party and government of Oceania through subversion, sabotage and terrorism.
3 Digital version of the book: http://www.mit.edu/hacker/part3.html, *op. cit.*

fighting illegal downloading, it has become a major geopolitical problem, encompassing malware infections, denial of service attacks (Distributed Denial of Service [DDoS]), security breach exploits, phishing, massive spam and targeted e-mail attacks, ransomware and "Trojan horse" type software, allowing large-scale criminal activities such as data theft, data blackmail, database destruction and serious disruption of the activities and functioning of the economy and public services. While acts of hacking have increased in the early years of the 21st Century, the end of the first decade of this new millennium has ushered cybercrime into a new era.

6.1.2. *When states engage in cyberwarfare*

Undoubtedly, Estonia's cyber-attack in 2007 marked the beginning of this new era. The attack came after the Estonian government decided to move the statue of the Bronze Soldier, a controversial monument to the memory of Soviet soldiers of the Second World War and considered by many Estonians as a symbol of the Soviet occupation. The removal of the statue from the center of Tallinn to the defense forces cemetery on the outskirts of the town provoked anger from the Russian minority in Estonia and the Russian government, who strongly condemned the decision and protested it, in a much less official and brutal way, by launching a cyber-attack on its small neighbor, carried out by Russian hackers from sites located on the outskirts of the Russian Federation. While the Estonian defense minister of the time was pleased that Estonia was "a world leader in the development of electronic services" – Estonia opted for a "paperless administration" and an almost complete computerization of its services – this innovative choice made it particularly vulnerable to computer attacks, as the DDoS attack on April 27 2007, a gigantic attack that paralyzed almost the entire country, suddenly revealed. Administrative, government and even large private company sites were shut down while their servers were flooded and rendered inoperative for several hours. After this new kind of attack, since it was the first time that state sites were targeted by such a large-scale operation, Estonia responded with attacks from its territory, targeting, for example, the Moscow radio station and *Kommersant*, one of the main Russian newspapers. Estonia and Russia, in doing so, inaugurated a new type of confrontation that the media soon dubbed as "cyberwar". The media often exaggerates. That was not the case this time. In 1993, in an article published by the RAND Corporation, the two researchers John Arquilla and David Ronfeldt already sounded the alarm: "Cyberwar is coming!"

However, this did not prevent the English political scientist Thomas Rid of King's College from proclaiming in 2011: "Today, cyberwar is more about hype than real risk" [RID 11].

Today, it is fair to say that Rid was overly optimistic in 2011. In 1999, two Chinese high-ranking officers, Qiao Liang and Wang Xiangsui, had already imagined the possibilities offered by cyber-weapons for espionage and the disruption of states and systems in a book entitled *Unrestricted Warfare* [QIA 06]. As early as 1999, China put the recommendations of the two officers into practice by launching cyber-attacks against the United States in response to the accidental bombardment of the Chinese embassy in Belgrade during military action that was conducted during the Serbian campaign. And in 2016, a report commissioned by the Pentagon from the RAND Corporation accurately assessed the challenges of cyberwarfare, which the authors consider to be a very concrete reality with potentially destructive consequences, since they conclude that the capabilities developed by the Chinese, in terms of digital warfare and cyberwarfare, would certainly enable the armed forces of the People's Republic of China to neutralize the U.S. Navy communication systems on a large scale and inflict very heavy casualties on U.S. forces [GOM 16].

The assertion, according to Thomas Rid, that cyberwarfare would not be able to cause damage in the physical world now seems to be seriously undermined. According to General Eric Bonnemaison, Deputy Director of Strategic Affairs at the French Ministry of Defense, "a faulty key can do more damage than a 250 kg bomb" [BOR 14]. Rid's main thesis in 2011 was that the cyberwarfare could only be virtual and conducted in an immaterial framework, which leads to dismissing many cases where the use of electronic weaponry took place in the context of military operations [BAU 12, pp. 305–316] and had very concrete consequences in the physical universe, as evidenced by the cyber-attack accompanying the Russian army's invasion of Georgia in 2008, which paralyzed Georgian communication systems. The effectiveness and scale of the cyber-attack this time further demonstrated that it was directly led by the Russian State and could be officially considered an act of war itself. In fact, even before Georgia, in October 2007 a virus of Israeli origin had rendered part of Syria's ground-to-air defenses inoperative, allowing Israeli aviation to bombard the Syrian nuclear reactor at Al-Kibar. In 2010, it was an attack using the Stuxnet worm that rendered an Iranian nuclear power plant inoperable.

6.1.3. *Computer attacks of an unprecedented magnitude*

A simple look back also reveals that this type of attack can be carried out on a large scale outside of a military context, and have severe consequences for civilian populations and the economy of a nation. The piracy of Sony in 2014, attributed by the United States to North Korea, was the worst piracy that a private company had ever experienced and led to the online broadcast of five films from the studio that had not yet been released in addition to the cancellation of the release of *The Interview*, the movie that was probably the source of the attack, which depicted Kim Jong-un's assassination. In addition to the estimated tens of millions of dollars in losses, the hacking led to the massive dissemination of e-mails, data and the personal addresses of Sony employees, data collected and uploaded by the WikiLeaks site. In January 2016, U.S. intelligence director James Clapper's telephone and Internet accounts (at Verizon) were hacked into. James Clapper's wife's Yahoo account was also hacked, while phone calls to the director of intelligence were diverted to the switchboard of a California-based Palestinian activist organization Free Palestine Movement. In April of the same year, 2.6 TB of data stolen from the Mossack Fonseca law firm caused the so-called "Panama Papers" case and, in the same month, a hacking into a database in Turkey led to the leak of the personal information of 50 million Turks. On May 18, 2016, the LinkedIn site announced that 100 million users' data had been stolen and, in June of the same year, it was Twitter's turn to announce the theft of 32 million identifiers.

But these large-scale attacks were nothing compared to the series that began in July 2016 with the WikiLeaks release of 20,000 stolen messages, following the hacking of the accounts of seven Democratic Party officials in the United States. The case took on such a scale, with suspicions bearing on Russia and accusations of collusion of Donald Trump's team with Russian circles, that it became potentially explosive for the American president. Had Donald Trump been far too close to the Russians or is he himself a victim of social engineering, the art of manipulation, which is the most basic and essential form of modern hacking, as Kevin Mitnick describes it in his book *The Art of Manipulation*? The affair worsened in August 2016 with the piracy of CNN and The New York Times, again reportedly carried out by Russian hackers. After the WikiLeaks Website publication of nearly 20,000 pirated messages from the accounts of seven Democratic Party officials, and the hacking of the intelligence director's telephone and Internet Verizon account, it became clear not only to the U.S. administration that Russia was seeking to interfere in the American election campaign through piracy, but even more so to the world that computer piracy was taking over the Internet.

Even the U.S. National Security Agency (NSA) was targeted and robbed, in August 2016 as well, from computer applications that were subsequently used in the May 2017 attacks. As pointed out by a researcher at Stanford University – one of three universities involved in the design and birth of ARPANET – Amy Zegart, cyberwarfare seems to be taking shape and having an impact on the physical world, particularly in environments as vulnerable as our connected societies. The main characteristic of this cyber warfare is that it concerns a huge surface area given that, according to Amy Zegart[4], there is on average a potential flaw in every 25–30 lines of code in a program, knowing that an operating system like Windows 7 has more than 40 million lines of code. With the rise of connected objects, the "battlefield" can grow in a very worrisome way and have serious repercussions in the physical world. Two examples were provided by the news of the DDoS attack launched from September 18–23 2016 against the French host OVH, by 146,000 surveillance cameras infected by a botnet, or the one launched, also from infected cameras, against the French viewing platform Dailymotion. The scale of the attacks is, once again, impressive. The DDoS attack on OVH peaked at one terabit per second on September 20, while the attack on Dailymotion resulted in 87.6 million personal accounts being hacked.

These attacks pale in comparison, however, with those that took place from May 12 to May 14 2017 and targeted more than 200,000 personal computers in more than 100 different countries with the help of the "WannaCry" ransomware, which has the effect of locking down the infected computer and sending the user a message requiring a ransom in exchange for the return of the data. This time, however, the attack was also launched against public institutions, including hospitals in the United Kingdom, which urgently had to cancel or postpone certain examinations and operations because of the amount of connected equipment rendered inoperative. Even the group of international hackers Anonymous resented it, notably Anonymous France, who published a message condemning the attacks and reproached the American NSA for having reported the theft, in its own databases, of the computer applications in question only after the May 12 attack began:

---

4 Amy Zegart, *Cyberwar*, TEDxStanford, http://ted.com/tedx.

The hackers are undoubtedly the "Shadow Brokers" who had previously stolen secret computer tools from the NSA, in addition, the famous Edward Snowden said: "If the NSA had debated in private about this flaw used to attack hospitals, when they 'discovered' it, rather than when it was stolen from them, it could have been avoided". However, the NSA had corrected the flaw before the group announced the theft of data, but the hack could not be avoided. (...) The virus exploits a Windows flaw, patches are available to protect itself for Windows Server 2003, Windows XP, Windows 8, perhaps also for Windows 7. It is therefore recommended to install the MS17-010 patch. WannaCry ransomware can even be stopped, in fact, MalwareTech discovered the address of a website in the software code. The virus tried to connect to this site when it was released; if the site was unreachable, it would continue to spread. Noting that the domain name was for sale, MalwareTech simply bought it, unknowingly activating the emergency mechanism that seemed to have been foreseen by the creators of the software and stopping its spread. In 2017, while some people want us to believe that it's almost impossible to hack or crack, we, Anonymous, want to remind you that no network will ever be 100% secure, just find the loophole and wait for the perfect moment[5].

Five days later, another attack of a similar magnitude took place, but with different objectives since the malware used, called Adylkuzz, simply uses the same flaw as WannaCry in order to hack into infected personal computers and force them to allocate part of their process capacity to mine Bitcoin and transfer the digital currency obtained to the anonymous accounts opened by the hackers. Once again, it was a computer tool stolen from the NSA that was used to attack on May 17.

6.1.4. *The darknet: cybercrime market*

Computer crime, hacking and the many forms of fraud that accompany it play an important role on the darknet. In a study conducted in January 2016, Daniel Moore and Thomas Rid [MOO 16, pp. 7–38] underline the multitude

5 Video published on YouTube by Anonymous France on May 13, 2017.

of Tor network sites offering this type of service: piracy, money laundering because of Bitcoin, trading in pirated credit card numbers and accounts and counterfeiting of banknotes, such as this counterfeit vendor cited in the article, insisting on reassuring its customers about its competence:

"Our banknotes are made of the highest quality cotton fiber. All security marks are included: watermark, microprint, colored ink, etc." [MOO 16, p. 10].

Figure 6.1. *Examples of services offered on .onion sites*

As can be seen in Figure 6.1, the Tor network offers genuine sales for operating faults, vulnerabilities, counterfeits and various hacks. Search engines such as Torch, like Grams for narcotics, allow you to expand or target your search in the field of Bitcoins and legal or illegal product markets.

The services offered on Tor in terms of piracy and fraud vary enormously, as do the justifications that accompany them, sometimes purely commercial, sometimes more political, such as the hacker who delivered the personal information of Venezuelan soldiers or FBI agents. However, compared to their predecessors and the cypherpunks of the 1990s, hackers today on the darknet (and on the Internet) show much more utilitarian motivations rather than ideological motivations, even though many sites on Tor, I2P and Freenet still develop a very "hacktivist" approach. Compared to the "heroic" times of the Legion of Doom and other net "supervisors", the darknet is a recruitment and trading platform on which competences are being seriously monetized, sometimes to the States themselves, as the examples mentioned above have shown. Cyberwarfare may not exist, but it is a growing professional sector.

6.2. Cybercrime, politics and subversion in the "half-world"

The specter of criminal activity on the darknet is not limited to piracy and drug trafficking. Violent crime and illegal pornography have attracted even more media attention. In the study cited in the previous section, "Cryptopolitik and the Darknet", Daniel Moore and Thomas Rid used a crawler, that is to say software programmed to connect to certain sites (here, those in .onion) in order to collect data and information, and index and categorize the largest number of sites for the purposes of study. According to a figure frequently used in Tor studies and reports, this network brings together between 45,000 and 60,000 sites, but without it being really possible to assess the validity of this assertion with any certainty. Moore and Rid based their study on the results provided by the search engines ahmia.fi and onion.city (now onion.link), establishing a list of over 5,000 sites from which their crawler extracted information that was then used to categorize the following activities: "Weapons", "Drugs", "Extremism", "Finance", "Hacking", "Illegal Pornography", "Nexus", "Other illegal", "Social", "Unknown", "Violence", "Other" and "None".

Alongside Websites dedicated to computer science or technical issues, and even hacking or computer and financial crime, online drug trafficking seems to be the most widespread activity on the Tor network. Out of a total of 5,205 sites visited and approximately 205,000 unique pages, as indicated by the authors of the study, the spyware returned the following results.

Category	Number of sites
None	2,482
Other	1,021
Drugs	423
Finance	327
Other illegal	198
Unknown	155
Extremism	140
Illegal pornography	122
Nexus	118
Hacking	96
Social	64
Weapons	42
Violence	17
Total	5,205
Total of active sites	2,723
Total of illegal sites	1,547

Table 6.1. *Typology of the 5,205 sites identified by the study*

However, the findings of the survey may be nuanced considering the results reported above. Indeed, the authors conclude that "the most common use of Tor's hidden services is criminal", a rather accurate assertion if one only considers sites whose activity have been precisely identified. Nevertheless, of the 5,205 sites visited, 2,482 are not classified in any category, 1,021 are identified as "Other", 327 are listed in the "Finance" category, which includes the mining of Bitcoins and other services that are not necessarily illegal. A further 155 sites fall into an "Unknown" category, 118 are placed in the "Nexus" category – which may include general forums and other meeting points around various topics – and 64 fall into the "Social" category. If we only retain the categories clearly identified as associated with criminal activity, a total of 1,038 out of 5,205 sites are left. The problem here is that some denominations remain very vague – "None",

"Other", "Unknown", "Nexus", "Social" – and these categories alone contain 3,840 sites distributed among them.

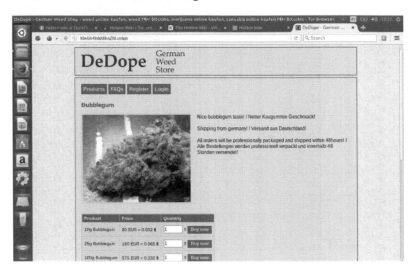

Figure 6.2. *Sites selling narcotic products*

This can be explained in several ways. The first explanation is that many of the sites hosted on the Tor network are actually inactive and are classified as "None" (2,482 sites), which is the overwhelming majority of the sites visited by the crawler. Another category includes forums and tutorials for newcomers on the darknet, as well as "Nexus" referring to forums that do not necessarily deal with illegal activities. Moreover, it should be added that institutions and major media have developed their own services on Tor, which clearly shows that they consider the services offered by Tor and its hidden network as a potential market and not an audience to be neglected. The same goes for Facebook, Twitter and *The New Yorker*, which now have their Tor services at their disposal, notably the *New Yorker* that offers The StrongBox, a secure document and testimonial repository service inspired by that of WikiLeaks, guaranteeing the anonymity of depositors. But many of the sites visited also require a registration procedure that prevents some people from knowing exactly what lies behind the home page and in which category to store them, which the authors place in the "Unknown" category. Among the sites directly linked to illegal activities, the sale of arms, narcotics, illegal pornography and violence (contract killers service, snuff movies, etc.) have particularly caught the attention of the media, and also hold a good place in Moore and Rid's study, not to mention the discussion groups and forums directed toward this type of practice. Moreover, we note that the Tor community does not unanimously tolerate this type of use, as demonstrated by the pedophile operation launched by Anonymous in 2013, or some sites of the network proposing to fight against child pornography sites by delivering, for example, the names or user IDs of their users when they can.

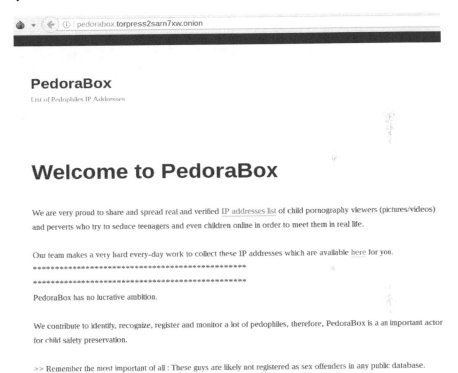

Figure 6.3. *Anti-pedopornographic site on Tor*

As far as violence is concerned, it is sometimes difficult to distinguish between real and fake in the services offered, for example, the Assassination Market site puts a price tag on the heads of the main heads of state. However, other examples seem to be much more serious, such as the one given by Moore and Rid, also from a site visited on the Tor network:

"We are a team of three contract killers operating in the United States (+ Canada) and Europe. As soon as you have placed your order, we will reply within 2-3 days, the contract will be executed in 1 to 3 weeks, depending on the target. Only rule: no children under 16 and no politicians in the top 10" [MOO 16].

6.2.1. *The "half-world" appeal*

Criminal activities, as long as they attract media attention, are not the only ones on darknets. The sociopolitical aspect of online activities should not be neglected either. The darknet has also been designed to give asylum to dissidents and minorities and to allow journalists to work more discreetly, in addition to also being a place of political activism: a plethora of alternative and conspiracy sites. Tor, the most frequented of the various darknets, is an ideal forum for the "democracy of the gullible", as evoked by Gérard Bronner in his eponymous work [BRO 13]. These sites express all the distrust felt toward governments, public authorities and representatives of authority. Edward Snowden is a recurring figure, sometimes also Hakim Bey, the author of *TAZ*, a reference widely shared by "darknauts".

Figure 6.4. *Alpha7 and Democracy now!, two political Websites (that are pro-Trump) on Tor*

This type of discourse is also found in sites that are not directly related to political issues or activism, but whose activity may be indirectly related to some form of activism or "hacktivism": hacking of course, but also illegal downloading – this type of service, which is curiously not raised by Moore and Rid, is everywhere on Tor, I2P and Freenet – and drug sales. Forums on such sites show that cybercrime is still frequently claimed to be a form of subversion, including the drug trade. An interesting study published in 2015 by A. Maddox, Monica J. Barratt, Matthew Allen and Simon Lenton, entitled "Constructive activism in the Darkweb" [MAD 15, pp. 111–126], offers an analysis centered on the famous Silk Road site, which was in the news in 2013 and 2014 after the arrest of its supposed founder and manager, Ross Ulbricht, and which has since managed to resurrect itself and find asylum on the I2P network, after being driven out of Tor. Now that we are familiar with the details of Silk Road's dealings with the FBI and the U.S. justice system, Maddox, Barratt, Allen and Lenton's study explores another aspect: the particular culture of Silk Road users, leading a number of online interviews between 2013 and 2014 in order to present an "ethnographic exploration of the original Silk Road", from which the authors deployed the concept of "constructive activism", that is to say a form of digital resistance to the institutions and the police force that some of the Silk Road users claim by engaging in the narcotics trade. This community of users found the opportunity to evoke its practices and consumption on the forum's hidden sites, such as Silk Road, all while intertwining their subversive approach with social and ideological claims. In this instance, the darknet offers the possibility of having an expression platform impossible to find on the clear web, much more regulated by the authorities and equally marked by an even stronger social control that is linked to the panoptism imposed by social networks. Since self-censorship is no longer practiced on darknet forums such as Silk Road, users not only express themselves completely freely about buying, selling and using drugs, but sometimes combine libertarian and anti-State considerations, encouraged by the moderators of the forums themselves. The opinions expressed thus strongly echo the views expressed by the cypherpunks in the 1990s, convinced that the joint use of cryptography and the Internet should lead to a complete reconfiguration of the relationship between the individual, society and the State. In Tim May and John Gilmore's time, this type of discourse already involved a joint and paradoxical exaltation of individualism and community. As Richard Barbrook notes, John Perry Barlow's declaration of independence in 1996 was already the outcome of a libertarian disillusionment: "At the moment when cyberspace was about to open up to the public, the personal freedom he cherished was about to be removed by legislation, without opposition. Unable to explain this phenomenon in California's ideological scheme, Barlow decided to escape into neoliberal hyper-reality" [BAR 01, p. 5].

Some of the discourses held on the darknet forums reflect the same disillusionment and the same desire to assert the existence of a "hyper-world" or a libertarian utopia, situated in an alternative reality where traditional powers can only intervene to a certain degree and where the norms imposed on the surface web, considered as the dominated digital space, no longer apply. In their study, Maddox, Barratt, Allen and Lenton note: "In response to this act of digital domination, acts of resistance are manifested, implying the creation of alternative spaces created through programming" [MAD 15, p. 113]. This type of attitude can be seen as manifestations of a new form of social activism, that is also based on a willingness to depersonalize, that goes against what social networks have imposed on the clear web. This is the implementation of what David Chaum considered in the 1980s as the liberation by username or avatar, in a cyberspace protected by encryption and anonymity. But this assertion of anonymized individualism does not prevent darknauts from simultaneously developing a very communitarian discourse that accredits the idea that the darknet is ultimately made up of communities, formed by the aggregation of virtual individuals, who have been united by technical capabilities and the will to escape from the alienating norms of the real world. Some of the statements made by Silk Road users in this regard point to post-teenage nostalgia:

> "What about the risk? Sometimes I miss the sensation of re-entering the "half-world" of the drug trade again (...) it's like reminding you of your college years, laughing at the memory of the dry spell you were in (...)" [MAD 15, p. 116]

In this virtual "Defense Zone", like Hakim Bey's "Temporary Autonomous Zone", the possession of technological know-how distinguishes an elite form of "darknauts", who recognize themselves in the use and animation of the hidden network, which is not open to everyone:

> "The dark web is unique in the sense that it is not particularly easy and well disposed towards the user. Technologies like Facebook or Twitter require five seconds to create an account and allow you to use all the features of the site. With Silk Road and other darknet markets, it's not so accessible. You need to learn how to encrypt and decrypt messages, and how to acquire a relatively esoteric virtual currency. And of course, these places aren't really well reported or even demonized in the media" [MAD 15, p. 116].

However, things could change because of a double evolution that affects the darknet today. The first factor of evolution is related to crime on hidden networks. At the beginning of the 2010s, public authorities and the media were still relatively unconcerned about the darknet, and even the FBI's high-profile intervention against Silk Road did not exactly take the Tor network out of confidentiality. Snowden's revelations have brought him a new popularity, but not in proportion to his use of the clear web. Things are changing today on the government side because, in the eyes of policy makers and governors, the darknet, and encryption solutions in general, are tools now used by terrorism to plan attacks and hit society. The *status quo* that prevailed, particularly after Tor's transition from government control to free licensing, is being challenged. In addition, the darknet itself, and the Tor network in particular, is gradually becoming more popular among Internet users. The demonstration has already been done with the creation of a Facebook on Tor, and even a Twitter in .onion.

Figure 6.5. *Twitter on Tor*

To conclude, we will therefore consider the very topical security issues that affect the darknet, but also the economic issues that may result from it, particularly with regard to the development of digital intelligence (DIGINT), in order to counter criminal and terrorist enterprises more effectively. Added to these challenges is the growing impact of not only networks, but also cryptographic currencies such as Bitcoin on the digital economy.

6.2.2. *Fighting crime and Bitcoins: current and future economic and security issues*

The questions faced by political authorities, international institutions, private operators and user communities with regard to the development of darknets are numerous. These include the development of a genuine digital and parallel economy based on the use of Bitcoin, the security and economic issues attached to it, but above all, and perhaps most importantly, the political issues linked to governance issues and the fear expressed by individuals that the Internet will become "fragmented" or "balkanized". Are these fears well founded, or is the development of darknets and a form of parallel digital economy merely proclaiming unavoidable economic transformations, spearheaded by virtual currencies, which have almost exclusively become the transaction tool of the darknet?

The *bit* of Bitcoin, which designates both the basic unit of measurement of information in computer language, as well as the binary logical alternative between 0 and 1, added to *coin* (which simply translates as a *currency*), is as a cryptographic currency and a peer-to-peer payment system pioneered by David Chaum with Digicash, created in 1994. Digicash was supposed to ensure the "non-traceability" of electronic transactions, but Chaum's company was declared bankrupt on November 4, 1998. However, successive contenders have emerged, such as the b-money concept, invented in November 1998 by the American computer engineer, and the claimed cypherpunk, Wei Dai, or the Bitgold concept, also invented by an American computer scientist named Nick Szabo in 1998. Wei Dai and Nick Szabo, both graduates of Washington University, did not have immediate success with their innovations, but they paved the way for the development of the Bitcoin. The creation of the current famous e-currency was claimed by the mysterious Satoshi Nakamoto in 2008. Behind this handle, there is likely to be different individuals involved in the development of the Bitcoin, whose operation is based on a "blockchain", in other words a set of relays allocating computational power in order to operate the encrypted currency transaction algorithm [REN 16].

The first Bitcoins were generated in 2009. At first, the virtual currency met with mixed success, initially arousing enthusiasm before facing a fall in its dollar exchange rate in 2011. As a decentralized trading system, Bitcoin is by nature the subject of intense speculative activity. Since its creation, the Bitcoin has consequently generated an early speculative bubble, raising the price of electronic money from 1 USD at the end of 2010, to 30 USD in June 2011. However, the bubble burst after this first rush, and the price dropped to 2 USD at the end of 2011. Slowly rising, the price of the Bitcoin rose to 20 USD in January 2013 and experienced a further surge to 266 USD on April 10, 2013, before the new speculative bubble burst once again and made Bitcoin fall below 50 USD by the end of 2013[6]. But the upsurge did not take long to resume from 2014 and despite significant fluctuations, the price of Bitcoin rose sharply to reach 20,000 USD on December 17, 2017, that is to say just over 16,000 EUR for a Bitcoin[7]. Despite the first negative prognoses generated by its high volatility, e-currency has thus experienced an impressive price surge, in addition to a significant increase in the amount of trading it makes possible. Key players in the real and digital economy have now adopted Bitcoin, such as Paypal, and in May 2014 the U.S. Federal Election Commission even approved Bitcoin as a means of financing campaigns. And Bitcoin is no longer alone. Now competing with other electronic currencies such as Monero or Zcash, Satoshi Nakamoto's creature no longer reigns supreme over the world of encrypted transactions. In August 2016, the online market Alphabay, which has a Website on both the Internet and the darknet, announced that it accepted Monero as a payment unit and also wished to integrate Zcash on July 1, 2017[8].

This craze for electronic currencies has several causes, including the development of encrypted networks and transactions on the Internet. As we have seen, electronic currencies, which are almost exclusively used on hidden networks as units of privileged transaction, are inseparable from the history of darknets. The fact that e-currency has become the preferred means of transaction and financing of illegal activities on the darknet is a major concern for authorities and security agencies today, particularly with regard to computer piracy, which has gone from activism to mercantile and capitalist logic in 20 years. Still largely ideologized and politicized in the 1990s, hacking is now a real market in perpetual expansion, as suggested by the series of ransomware attacks in May and June 2017. Perhaps even more so than criminal activities such as drug trafficking or child pornography, piracy is becoming the main concern of intelligence agencies, and security

---

6 Source: https://www.mataf.net/fr/bourse/edu/investissement/l-evolution-du-cours-du-bitcoin-depuis-sa-creation.
7 2506.97 USD and 2209.66 EUR on June 28, 2017, https://bitcoin.fr/cours-du-bitcoin/.
8 https://www.wedemain.fr/Monero-cette-nouvelle-crypto-monnaie-qui-concurrence-le-Bitcoin-sur-le-darknet_a2091.html/https://alphabaymarket.com/alphabay-accept-zcash-payment-soon/.

and police services, especially since piracy can not only be linked to criminal motives and the search for fraudulent benefit, but can also be a very effective destabilization tool in the hands of malicious individuals and various organizations, whether or not in the service of States. As the attacks of May and June 2017 showed, and as already amply demonstrated by the cyber-attacks in 2007 and 2008 against Estonia and Georgia, it is quite possible to paralyze public service functions, whole administrations and large institutions or companies. Neither can we reject the idea that some terrorist groups may be able to use this weapon much more effectively to carry out psychological warfare actions with very concrete repercussions in the real world, potentially costing human lives if certain sensitive installations are targeted. Particularly in the case of the Islamic State, Western security services are concerned about the possibility of the terrorist organization, which is in full disarray in Syria and Iraq, withdrawing into cyberspace by continuing to virtually inhabit the "Cyber Caliphat", proclaimed at the same time as the birth of the Islamic State in 2014, in particular on the darknet. The fear of counterterrorism authorities and institutions is also that the darknet's sites and forums will serve as platforms for exchanging sensitive data and software that can be used to carry out larger scale destabilization actions. As revealed in *How to survive in the West: A Mujahid Guide*, published in 2015 on the Internet[9], Islamist terrorist organizations have recently become aware of the opportunity offered by networks such as Tor, which have now reached a level of development sufficient to generate "noise" and attendance that can provide enough coverage for the preparation of terrorist activities, in addition to the relative anonymity offered by encrypted networks. The *Mujahid Guide* includes sections entitled *Bomb Making* and *Weapon Training*, as well as a chapter on the use of Tor for communication, anonymous exchanges and preparation of operations, in addition to the dissemination of jihadist propaganda [WEI 16, p. 198]. During his trial in 2015, Ali Shukri Amin[10], arrested in the United States in 2015, admitted that Tor's hidden sites and forums offered freedom of exchange and communication that allowed him to undertake a more productive and much less risky recruitment job than on a Facebook group or a clear web forum. Similarly, the Al-Hayat Media Center, the Islamic State's news and propaganda body, told its visitors how to move from sites neutralized by the authorities or by "Operation Paris", launched by the

9 And whose PDF version is easy to find online: https://www.blazingcatfur.ca/wp-content/uploads/2015/04/ISIS-How-to-survive-in-the-west.pdf.
10 A 17-year-old teenager tried and sentenced for "active support to a terrorist organization" after joining the Islamic State organization online and helping a comrade to leave for Syria.

Anonymous group on Tor after the attacks in Paris in November 2015. In February 2015, a report by Michael Chertoff and Tobby Simon already suggested the following measures to combat the displacement of terrorist and propaganda activities on the Tor network:

1) infiltrate the hash table, in other words the directory that distributes data storage and associates it with keys on Tor or I2P network nodes, in an attempt to identify suspicious traffic, sites and accounts;

2) analyze data from access providers in order to identify connections to "non-standard" domains (in other words: .onion addresses);

3) infiltrate suspect sites' forums on Tor and analyze exchanges to identify potential threats;

4) establish an effective typology of the different markets present on the darknet and try to identify sensitive exchanges [CHE 16].

As Chertoff and Simon also note in their report, the development of darknets has longer term paradoxical consequences for the digital economy, cybersecurity and Internet governance. One of the first consequences is the concurrent development of a true cybersecurity economy, in both the public and private sectors, which attempts to respond to new threats by providing public services, as well as private companies, with analytical and protective tools in order to counter the threats posed by both piracy and terrorism. These tools include the development and use of data mining, deepnet mining and darknet mining tools to conduct preventive intelligence activities. Some universities, particularly in the United States, are heavily invested in this type of research and development work related to finding answers to the new problems raised by the emergence of darknets. In a study published in July 2016, researchers at Arizona State University [NUN 16] presented a referencing tool focused on dark and deepnet mining, whose prototype was able to identify more than 300 serious threats per week, collected because of a computerized data collection tool quite similar to the one experimented by Thomas Rid's team [MOO 16]. "We provide this information to cybersecurity professionals in order to contribute to their cyber defense strategy", say the study's authors, who use data extraction and classification software in order to particularly monitor and analyze the traffic and exchanges taking place on exchange platforms and forums hosted on the Tor network. In the same way as Google's anti-spam service, researchers use the latest machine learning and artificial intelligence technologies to refine their searches and make these tools as efficient as possible. The study thus provides a very good example of cooperation between the academic and scientific community, and public and private sectors, in what is gradually expanding as a global market for cybersecurity.

This is only one aspect of the profound changes taking place today in the digital economy and which are linked to the development of cryptography on the Internet. As Michael Chertoff notes, governments and authorities grappling with criminal behavior and the terrorist risk on the darknet today have a global choice between two attitudes: direct control, or even interruption of traffic – the kill switch used by the Egyptian government during the Arab Spring events, and which the London municipality was itself tempted to use during the 2011 riots, or digital surveillance and intelligence, carried out in a more discreet manner. In the first case, which is often the option favored by authoritarian or semiauthoritarian States, the risk is to damage the cyberspace ecosystem while only displacing the threat. In the second case, the difficulty lies in the enormous volume of data to be processed, which now explains the resort to using data mining and deepnet mining tools that are still in the development and experimentation phase. "The most effective way, "says Chertoff", is to search for illegal sites rather than illegal users. With legal authorization, government hackers may place de-anonymization tools on relays, nodes or computers accessing these sites. If the authorities close down the sites in question, they will reappear elsewhere. On the other hand, if authorities incriminate users, others may be reluctant to use such sites in the future because of the risk involved. The final option could be to break Tor, in order to identify each user. This would result, as the Silk Road case has shown, in pushing for a more robust version of Tor, which would ruin the authorities' efforts. It would also risk destroying a very useful tool for dissidents" [CHE 17, p. 36].

This analysis reflects the complex and contradictory reality of darknets, and in particular Tor, given the public success of this network: on the one hand, absolute anonymity remains a decoy, given that the public authorities have the technical means to de-anonymize part of the traffic. On the other hand, given the use of networks such as Tor, it becomes inconceivable to de-anonymize all traffic, as successive software versions are increasingly resistant to attacks. Tor was born in government, but it seems to have escaped its creator at the present day, not only on a political, but a technical level as well. This state of affairs even leads public authorities and private companies to consider migrating certain services to Tor, whose architecture is proving extremely resilient [JAR 15]. It would therefore be necessary for authorities and state powers to follow the path opened by some major private operators in the digital economy, and to not just consider Tor as a potential threat and a space to be monitored, but also as a more secure service platform solution than the clear web. It would be like closing the loop, since Tor was first developed to provide a secure communication space for government services. However, this is not yet the case today: navigation on the Tor network would have to be made much simpler and more attractive for the general public to really turn to this solution and make sure that, as journalist Jamie Bartlett put it, "Tor becomes mainstream"[11].

---

11 https://www.ted.com/talks/jamie_bartlett_how_the_mysterious_dark_net_is_going_mainst ream.

Conclusion

The darknet model defined by Peter Biddle, Paul England, Marcus Peinado and Bryan William in 2003 has evolved considerably over the past 14 years. From the transposition of splinter net models to peer-to-peer architecture, with the development of Tor, I2P and Freenet, we have moved on to true parallel networks, integrated into the network of Internet networks, yet operating autonomously and semi-autonomously on the basis of an electronic addressing and file exchange protocol that is specific to each of these encrypted networks. These developments, as well as the relative success of these hidden networks, particularly Tor, raise new questions in many areas and put under scrutiny the concept of Internet governance, which ICANN has been debating for several years. The emergence and rise in power of darknets could significantly change the terms of the debate, or at least bring new lines of thought.

However, the prospect of seeing encrypted networks develop leads to another question, deliberately controversial in the title of Milton Mueller's latest work, published in 2017: *Will the Internet Fragment?* [MUE 17]. Faced with pressure from various governments, demanding ways of adapting the Internet to national legislation and the temptation of some user communities to use cryptography to make a literal "secession", the fear of the Internet's "balkanization" looms. Even cybersecurity expert Eugene Kapersky proclaims that "the fragmentation of the Internet will cause a paradoxical deglobalization of the world" [MUE 17, p. 11]. However, the fragmentation of the Internet is already in effect. It has been even since the creation of this "network of networks", made up of a multitude of autonomous and semiautonomous wholes. However, all of these wholes use a common *lingua franca*, which is the TCP/IP protocol. Yet the appearance and development of .onion sites have undermined this principle, given that it defines the existence of spaces where the protocol used is different and effectively prohibits interoperability between most of the services of the surface web and darknets. Nevertheless, the concern for interoperability seems to triumph with the development of software solutions such as Tor2Web, which now even allows the progressive referencing of sites in .onion in Google. It must be admitted, however, that some of the hidden services offered by darknets have withdrawn for good on Tor, I2P an Freenet, and no longer speak the same *lingua franca* to the rest of the Internet.

The fear of witnessing the fragmentation of the Internet is also heightened by the willingness of States to secure greater control over traffic, or even to create, as China proposed in 2012, real DNS and national domains, operating somewhat like telephone codes. While the Chinese proposal has never been accepted by ICANN's bodies, the issue remains unresolved and there is still great concern that there will be a gradual split between "digital lawless zones" and an Internet reappropriated by states. The NETMundial meeting in Sao Paulo in April 2014 was thus marked by Edward Snowden's revelations and fears. Fadi Chehadé, who was already ICANN's president at the time, made it clear that there was a danger of uncontrolled development linked to non-negotiated governance: "If we cannot find a fair way to govern the Internet, we risk regressing to a form of fragmentation" [MUE 17, p. 12].

The development of the Internet by the U.S. Department of Defense aimed to provide its field agents with interoperability and connectivity that was independent of the hardware used. The development of this principle has surpassed the ambitions – and control – of the military authorities. From the time that the use of personal computers began to spread, the need for universal protocols became global. The emergence of this concept has created its own limitations given that cyberspace, like any other space, offers a field of development for criminal and illegal activities that the user must have the means to obstruct or at least protect himself from. This necessity gives rise to a paradox: that of the global nature of the Internet, confronted with the national nature of the courts sanctioning and controlling the various misuses, a contradiction that appears from the origins of the Internet. The institutional response still does not exist and this contradiction is perfectly illustrated by the current challenges of cybersecurity. For many state operators, Snowden's revelations showed that the globalized Internet exchange space was still subject to the supremacy of the United States, which led to the emergence of a pure free trade area and a perfect tool for rationalizing and controlling information. For others, this has led to the realization that the network's neutrality and freedom may be compromised in the near future, and that tools and policies must be developed to preserve it, such as what "hacktivist" John Perry Barlow called for in his "Declaration of Independence from Cyberspace" in 1996.

Therefore, the development of darknets is fully in line with the debate on Internet governance as this phenomenon, which is part of a major evolution of digital technologies, is linked to major problems that are also at the heart of the concerns of the various governments on the planet with regard to the Internet: security and cybersecurity, the alignment of the Internet with national jurisdictions and, conversely, the possibility of partially escaping legislative and legal constraints, and the maintenance of a common protocol that always ensures universal interoperability of systems. Will darknets announce major changes in terms of uses and digital economy in the near future? In any case, the phenomenon is far from being reduced to cybercrime, but does give us a glimpse of the face of the Internet as it might appear in the years to come: an Internet that may be more fragmented by political will, more compartmentalized by the use of cryptography and offering new digital territories to explore; it is still too early to say. Either way, it is certain that our relationship with this virtual universe is drastically evolving once again. In this rapidly evolving context, the darknet is far from being a mere virtual territory in which new forms of cybercrime develop, however spectacular they may be. The "dark Internet" has a broader role to play in the evolution of the Internet, from network governance issues to new opportunities for users. The future of the Internet may now lie in the hidden side of the network.

APPENDICES

Appendix 1

Declaration of Independence of Cyberspace (John P. Barlow, February 1996)[1]

Just over 20 years ago, on February 8 1996, essayist John Perry Barlow, a former writer for the Grateful Dead and co-founder of the Electronic Frontier Foundation, wrote the "Declaration of Independence of Cyberspace" in response to the 1996 enactment of the Telecommunications Act in the United States, which Barlow considered liberticidal. The document reproduced below corresponds to the original text posted on the Internet. It contains Barlow's foreword and the declaration itself.

> Yesterday, the great invertebrate in the White House signed the Telecom "Reform" Act of 1996, while Tipper Gore took digital photos of the event to include them in a book called *24 Hours in Cyberspace*.
>
> I was also asked to participate in the creation of this book by writing something appropriate to the circumstances. Given the horror this legislation would inflict on the Internet, I thought it would be a good time to show some resistance.
>
> After all, the Telecom "Reform" Act, which passed the Senate with only four votes against, makes it illegal, and punishable by a $250,000 fine, to say "shit" online. Like saying one of the

1 Original text on the EFF Website, February 9, 1996.

seven words forbidden in mainstream media. And discuss abortion openly. And to talk about physical functions other than in purely clinical terms.

This legislation seeks to impose stronger constraints on conversation in cyberspace than those that exist today in the Senate cafeteria, where I have heard colored indecency from U.S. senators every time I have had dinner.

This law has been implemented against us by people who have no idea who we are, or where our conversations are being conducted. It is, as my friend and editor-in-chief of Wired Louis Rosseto said, as if "illiterates told you what you could read".

Well, fuck them.

Or, more appropriately, let us take leave of them. They declared war on the Network. Let us show them how clever, confusing and powerful we can be to defend ourselves.

I have written something (with all the relevant detail) that I hope will become one of the means to this end. If you find it useful, I hope you will pass it on as widely as possible. You can omit my name if you like, because I do not care if someone credits me with the text. I really don't.

But what I hope is that this clamor will find traction in the Network, changing, growing and multiplying, until it becomes a great commotion equal to the cretinism that has just been inflicted on us.

Here it is...:

Declaration of independence of cyberspace

"Only error needs government support. The truth can handle itself".

(Thomas Jefferson, *Notes on Virginia*)

Governments of the Industrial World, you weary giants of flesh and steel, I come from Cyberspace, the new home of

Mind. On behalf of the future, I ask you of the past to leave us alone. You are not welcome among us. You have no sovereignty where we gather.

We have no elected government, nor are we likely to have one, so I address you with no greater authority than that with which liberty itself always speaks. I declare the global social space we are building to be naturally independent of the tyrannies you seek to impose on us. You have no moral right to rule us nor do you possess any methods of enforcement we have true reason to fear.

Governments derive their just powers from the consent of the governed. You have neither solicited nor received ours. We did not invite you. You do not know us, nor do you know our world. Cyberspace does not lie within your borders. Do not think that you can build it, as though it were a public construction project. You cannot. It is an act of nature and it grows itself through our collective actions.

You have not engaged in our great and gathering conversation, nor did you create the wealth of our marketplaces. You do not know our culture, our ethics, or the unwritten codes that already provide our society more order than could be obtained by any of your impositions.

You claim there are problems among us that you need to solve. You use this claim as an excuse to invade our precincts. Many of these problems don't exist. Where there are real conflicts, where there are wrongs, we will identify them and address them by our means. We are forming our own Social Contract. This governance will arise according to the conditions of our world, not yours. Our world is different.

Cyberspace consists of transactions, relationships and thought itself, arrayed like a standing wave in the web of our communications. Ours is a world that is both everywhere and nowhere, but it is not where bodies live.

We are creating a world that all may enter without privilege or prejudice accorded by race, economic power, military force or station of birth.

We are creating a world where anyone, anywhere may express his or her beliefs, no matter how singular, without fear of being coerced into silence or conformity.

Your legal concepts of property, expression, identity, movement and context do not apply to us. They are all based on matter, and there is no matter here.

Our identities have no bodies, so, unlike you, we cannot obtain order by physical coercion. We believe that from ethics, enlightened self-interest, and the commonweal, our governance will emerge. Our identities may be distributed across many of your jurisdictions. The only law that all our constituent cultures would generally recognize is the Golden Rule. We hope we will be able to build our particular solutions on that basis. But we cannot accept the solutions you are attempting to impose.

In the United States, you have today created a law, the Telecommunications Reform Act, which repudiates your own Constitution and insults the dreams of Jefferson, Washington, Mill, Madison, DeToqueville and Brandeis. These dreams must now be born anew in us.

You are terrified of your own children, since they are natives in a world where you will always be immigrants. Because you fear them, you entrust your bureaucracies with the parental responsibilities you are too cowardly to confront yourselves. In our world, all the sentiments and expressions of humanity, from the debasing to the angelic, are parts of a seamless whole, the global conversation of bits. We cannot separate the air that chokes from the air upon which wings beat.

In China, Germany, France, Russia, Singapore, Italy and the United States, you are trying to ward off the virus of liberty by erecting guard posts at the frontiers of Cyberspace. These may keep out the contagion for a small time, but they will not work in a world that will soon be blanketed in bit-bearing media.

Your increasingly obsolete information industries would perpetuate themselves by proposing laws, in America and elsewhere, that claim to own speech itself throughout the world. These laws would declare ideas to be another industrial product, no more noble than pig iron. In our world, whatever the human mind may create can be reproduced and distributed infinitely at no cost. The global conveyance of thought no longer requires your factories to accomplish.

These increasingly hostile and colonial measures place us in the same position as those previous lovers of freedom and self-determination who had to reject the authorities of distant, uninformed powers. We must declare our virtual selves immune to your sovereignty, even as we continue to consent to your rule over our bodies. We will spread ourselves across the Planet so that no one can arrest our thoughts.

We will create a civilization of the Mind in Cyberspace. May it be more humane and fair than the world your governments have made before.

Davos, Switzerland
February 8, 1996

Appendix 2

Digital Gangster Manifesto

There are few times when it is essential to wake up. That time has come.

You don't have to wait until someone wakes you up. You are the lunatics, the social cases, the rebels, the troublemakers, the ones who see things differently.

We are not in love with rules and we have no respect for statuary.

You can imprison and oppress us, we don't care because we are legion.

The only thing you can't do is ignore us, because we are making a difference. We create revolutions, we create a free society here and now.

And while they fear us, with their nepotism and kleptocracy,

Their bureaucracy and ideology, and their police and spies calling us criminals,

We see nothing but creation.

Because the ones who are crazy enough

To think they can change the world

Are the ones who do it.

But have you, in your nepotism and your 20th kleptocracy, ever

Seen things through the eyes of a hacker? Have you ever wondered

What made him move forward, what forces shaped him?

We are hackers, we create, enter our world.

We found a computer. Wait a minute, that's cool.

It does what it's told to do. If it makes a mistake,

That's because we screwed up. Not because it doesn't like us...

Or feels like we're threatening it...

Or thinks we're smartasses...

Or don't like teaching and shouldn't be here...

And then it happened... A door to a world opened...

We run across the Internet like heroin runs through the veins of a drug addict,

An electronic pulse resonates, a refuge is found against the nonsense of everyday life...

A lifeline.

"It's here... it's where I belong..."

We know everyone here... even though we've never met, nor talked.

Even though we've never heard of them... We all know you....

You talk as if we're all the same... We were stuffed with baby food at school when we were salivating at the sight of a steak...

The pieces of meat you dropped were minced and bland.

We have been dominated by sadists, and ignored by apathetic people.

The few who had something to teach us found volunteers in us,

But these few were but drops of water in the desert.

Life is nothing more than a drop in a boundless ocean.

But what is an ocean

But a multitude of drops?

It's our world now... the world of the electron and the switch,

The beauty of 0 and 1. We took advantage of an existing service without paying for what could have been cheap, if it wasn't being run by profiting gluttons, and you call us criminals.

We explore... and you call us criminals. We are looking for knowledge...

and you call us criminals. We exist without skin color, without nationality,

Without religious bias... and you call us criminals.

You build atomic bombs, you start wars,

You murder, you cheat and you lie to us to try and make us believe

That all this is for our own good, but once again, we are the criminals.

Yeah, I'm a criminal. My crime is curiosity.

My crime is to judge people for what they say or do,

Not what they look like.

My crime is to be smarter than you, something you'll never forgive.

I'm a hacker and this is my manifesto. You can arrest this individual,

But you won't stop us all... after all: we are all alike.

#SailSafeMotherFuckers!

Source: Home page of the Digital Gangster Website,
Tor network

Glossary

AFNIC: *French Association for Cooperative Internet Naming (Association française pour le nommage Internet en cooperation).* Non-profit organization whose mission is to manage the first level Internet domains in metropolitan France and overseas and in the French Southern and Antarctic Lands.

Anonymous: An activist movement created around 2003–2004, bringing together an international nebula of more or less active groups, claiming to be active in the defense of freedom of expression, a struggle to which are added a wide variety of political demands.

ARPANET: *Advanced Research Projects Agency Network.* First packet data transfer network developed by DARPA from 1969 to 1972.

Backbone: Backbones are the first and most important long-distance computer networks, to which the multiple networks that make up the Internet today have been added.

Big Data: The term, which appeared in the 1990s and became popular in the second half of the 2010s, refers to the creation of very large volumes of data, concurrent with the development of the Internet. The management of Big Data is seen as one of the main challenges of the coming decade in scientific, commercial and cybersecurity fields.

Bitcoin: Virtual and cryptographic currency distributed since 2009, the operation of which is based on a decentralized network of nodes that provides transaction processing and enables users allocating computing power to be remunerated. Bitcoin theoretically allows secure and anonymous payment transactions, hence its success on darknets.

Connected objects: The "Internet of Things" [IoT] represents all connected objects capable of exchanging information on the Internet from the real world. The extension of the IoT to many everyday consumer items such as cars, household appliances, surveillance cameras and telephones represents, for specialists, a new revolution in information and communication technologies called "Web 3.0", after "Web 1.0" (after Lee and Cailliau invented the World Wide Web) and "Web 2.0" (the rise of social networks).

Cybersecurity: A set of laws, policies, tools, devices, concepts, technologies and methods of security that can be used to protect people and tangible and intangible computer assets.

Darknet/darknets: The term "darknets" was used for the first time in an article published by Microsoft engineers Peter Biddle, Paul England, Marcus Peinado and Bryan Willman. It refers to any type of parallel network that is encrypted or requires a specific protocol to allow a user to connect to it. Tor and I2P are considered darknets. In the singular, the term darknet refers more generically to all the hidden networks whose architecture is superimposed on that of the Internet.

DARPA: *Defense Advanced Project Research Agency.* American research agency dependent on the Department of Defense (DoD), which supervised the first phase of development of ARPANET, then the Internet.

DB: Database.

Deep web: The term deep web, popularized in the media since the middle of the first decade of the 21st Century, refers to all databases built up on the Internet since its creation and its release to the general public. The deep web, which is therefore a much larger whole than the surface web, should not be confused with darknet, which designates hidden networks, or the dark web, which refers to the databases and interfaces accessible only on these hidden networks.

Domain: In computing, a domain is a network of computers connected together to the Internet. For example, a domain such as .fr is all computers hosting activities for individuals or organizations that have registered with the French Association for Cooperative Internet Naming (AFNIC). The DNS

(Domain Name System) is the global domain name directory managed by ICANN and IANA.

EFF: *Electronic Frontier Foundation.* An international NGO dedicated to the protection of freedoms on the Internet, based in San Francisco and founded in 1990 by Mitch Kapor, John Gilmore and John Perry Barlow. EFF has taken over the management of the Tor project since it left the U.S. military.

FTP: *File Transfer Protocol.* A protocol for transferring and sharing files over a network that allows files to be copied to one computer from another on the network.

GAFTA: Acronym for the giants of the digital economy: Google, Apple, Facebook, Twitter, Amazon. We also talk about GAFA, by omitting Twitter, or GAFAM, including Microsoft.

gTLD: *generic Top Level Domain.* Example: Domains registered in .com or .org.

HTTP: *HyperText Transfer Protocol.* Server-to-client data transfer protocol developed for the World Wide Web. The HTTPS (*HyperText Transfer Protocol Secured*) is a secure version of this protocol.

IANA: *Internet Assigned Numbers Authority.* A private U.S. non-profit organization that oversees the global allocation of IP address, autonomous system number allocation and root zone management in the Domain Name System (DNS).

ICANN: *Internet Corporation for Assigned Names and Numbers.* International organization responsible for overseeing the assignment of IPv4 and IPv6 addresses and Internet domain names.

Internet: A global computer network, often referred to as the "network of networks", given that it brings together more than 50,000 subnetworks, which are themselves subdivided into a multitude of subsections and autonomous networks.

IETF: *Internet Engineering Task Force.* An international organization dedicated to the technical development of Internet communication standards and protocols.

Internet Society (ISOC): An international organization established under American law in 1992 in order to develop and coordinate computer networks worldwide. ISOC, like ICANN, is one of the institutions dedicated to global Internet governance.

IPv4: *Internet Protocol version 4.* This is the first version of *Internet Protocol*, published in 1981, which allowed the assignment of 32-bit encrypted IP addresses. IPv4 is still widely used in 2017, although the number of possible combinations was officially exhausted on February 3, 2011.

IPv6: The successor to IPv4, developed by the *Internet Engineering Task Force* (IETF) in 1998. IPv6 offers 128-bit addresses, which provides a much larger pool of IP addresses than IPv4. However, since IPv6 is not an IPv4 compatible protocol, its use is still very limited in 2017.

Librenet: The term can refer to the culture of open source software on the Internet, but also to the guarantee of anonymity and privacy, notably through networks such as Freenet. Since March 2017, Librenet has also been a secure parallel network project, whose financing is being launched on the Kickstarter platform.

Newsgroups: System of data exchange and communication through forums, the first model of which was USENET developed in 1979.

NSA: *National Security Agency.* Created at the end of the Second World War, this American intelligence agency which specializes in electromagnetic and electronic intelligence, cryptography and the processing of information systems, found itself in the spotlight in June 2013 after Edward Snowden, ex-agent of the NSA, revealed the system of large-scale espionage, set up by the NSA to spy on American citizens and allied countries.

Open source: In other words, "open source code". A term for any software whose source code is made available to the general public and is freely distributed.

P2P: *Peer-to-peer.* A computer network model, in which each client is also a server, which can be used to exchange files and data of all types.

Proxy: The proxy is software or a computer component that acts as an intermediary to monitor or secure the connection between two hosts. A server can, by extension, be considered a proxy.

Server: A computer unit or workstation that physically hosts the data enabling, for example, a Website to be placed on the Internet.

Silk Road: Online drug dealer on the Tor network, dismantled by the FBI in October 2013, then November 2014.

Surface web: The surface web that includes all commonly used applications, sites and databases easily accessible from a simple search on a conventional search engine.

TCP/IP: *Transfer Control Protocol/Internet Protocol.* The set of protocols used for transferring and exchanging data over the Internet.

Tor: *The Onion Router.* The Tor project was first developed in the late 1990s under the aegis of the U.S. Army and then freely distributed in the early 2000s. The Tor project offers an anonymized browser, the Tor Browser Bundle and a site creation service in .onion, which is, strictly speaking, the Tor darknet.

VPN: *Virtual Private Network.*

WHOIS: *"Who is?".* Worldwide domain name registry search service.

WWW: *World Wide Web.* The "spiderweb", the web, is a hypertext system running on the Internet, allowing one, through a browser, to browse pages and Websites hosted on the global network. The World Wide Web was created by Tim Berners-Lee and Robert Cailliau in 1990.

Bibliography

[AND 04] ANDROUTSELLIS-THEOTOKIS S., SPINELLIS D., "A survey of peer-to-peer content distribution technologies", *ACM Computing Surveys*, vol. 36, no. 4, pp. 335–371, 2004.

[ARQ 97] ARQUILLA J., RONFELDT D., "Cyberwar is coming!", in ARQUILLA J., RONFELDT D. (eds), *In Athena's Camp: Preparing for Conflict in the Information Age*, RAND, Santa Monica, California, 1997.

[BAL 13] BALL J., SCHNEIER B., GREENWALD G., "NSA and GCHQ target Tor network that protects anonymity of web users", *The Guardian*, 2013.

[BAR 96] BARLOW J.P., "Déclaration d'indépendance du cyberespace", available at : http://editions-hache.com/essais/barlow/barlow2.html, 1996.

[BAR 01] BARBROOK R., LUDLOW P. (eds), *Crypto Anarchy, Cyberstates and Pirate Utopias*, MIT Press, Cambridge, 2001.

[BAR 13] BARLOW J.P., "I am John Perry Barlow, cofounder of the *Electronic Frontier Foundation,* lyricist for *the Grateful Dead.* My most recent work is with the Freedom of the Press Foundation. Ask me anything", available at: https://www.reddit.com/ r/IAmA/comments/1kgmes/i_am_john_perry_barlow_cofounder_of_the/, 2013.

[BAR 14] BARTLETT J., *The Dark Net: Inside the Digital Underworld*, Random House, 2014.

[BAU 00] BAUMAN Z., *Liquid Times: Living in an Age of Uncertainty*, Polity Press, Cambridge, 2000.

[BAU 12] BAUD M., "La cyberguerre n'aura pas lieu, mais il faut s'y préparer", *Politique étrangère*, vol. 2, pp. 305–316, 2012.

[BER 99] BERNERS-LEE T., *Weaving the Web: The Original Design and Ultimate Destiny of the World Wide Web by Its Inventor,* Harper Business, 1999.

[BER 01] BERTHOLD O., FEDERRATH H., KÖPSELL S., "Web MIXes: a system for anonymous and unobservable web access", *Proceeding of the Workshop on Design Issues in Anonymity and Unobservability,* Berkeley, 2001.

[BEY 91] BEY H., "TAZ, Temporary Autonomous Zone. Ontological Anarchy, Poetic Terrorism", available at: http://lyber-eclat.net/lyber/taz.html, 1991.

[BID 03] BIDDLE P., ENGLAND P., PEINADO M. *et al.*, "The darknet and the future of content distribution", Microsoft Corporation, available at: *http://msl1.mit.edu/ESD10/docs/darknet5.pdf*, 2003.

[BLU 83a] BLUM M., "Coin flipping by telephone: a protocol for solving impossible problems", ACM SIGACT News, vol. 15, no. 1, 1983.

[BLU 83b] BLUM M., "How to exchange (secret) keys", ACM Transactions on Computer System, vol. 1, no. 2, pp. 175–193, 1983.

[BOR 14] BORIES C., "Appréhender la cyberguerre en droit international, Quelques réflexions et mises au point", *La Revue des droits de l'homme* [e-journal], vol. 6, cited by Clémentine BORIES, "Appréhender la cyberguerre en droit international, available at : http://revdh.revues.org/984, 2014.

[BOR 16] BOREL S., "Le panoptisme horizontal ou le panoptisme inversé", *tic&société*, vol. 10, no. 1, 2016.

[BRO 13] BRONNER G., *La démocratie des crédules*, PUF, 2013.

[CAM 01] CAMPBELL D., *Surveillance électronique planétaire*, Éditions Allia, 2001, republished in 2007.

[CAS 13] CASILLO I., "Espace public", in CASILLO I., BARBIER R., BLONDIAUX L. *et al*, (dir.), *Dictionnaire critique et interdisciplinaire de la participation*, GIS Démocratie et Participation, Paris, 2013.

[CHA 81a] CHAUM D.L., "Blind signatures and untraceable payments", *Advances in Cryptology Proceedings*, vol. 82, no. 3, pp. 199–203, 1981.

[CHA 81b] CHAUM D.L., "Untraceable electronic mail, return addresses and digital pseudonyms", *Communications of the ACM*, vol. 24, no. 2, 1981.

[CHA 85] CHAUM D.L., "Security without identification: transaction systems to make Big Brother obsolete", *Communications of the ACM*, vol. 28, no. 10, 1985.

[CHA 16] CHAFFIN Z., "Paris dénonce une "privatisation" de la gouvernance d'Internet", Le Monde, available at: http://www.lemonde.fr/economie/article/2016/03/24/icann-paris-denonce-une-privatisation-de-la-gouvernance-d-internet_4889567_3234.html, 2016.

[CHE 16] CHERTOFF M., SIMON T., "The impact of the Dark Web on Internet Governance and cyberSecurity", available at: www.cigionline.org/sites/default/files/gcig_paper_no6.pdf, 2016.

[CHE 17] CHERTOFF M., "A public policy perspective of the Dark Web", *Journal of Cyber Policy*, vol. 2, no. 1, 2017.

[CHO 93] CHOLLET L., "William Gibson's Second Sight", *Los Angeles Times*, 1993.

[CHR 15] CHRISTIE M.-J., "David Chaum and Ecash: privacy technology's negociations of political, cultural, and techno-social contingencies in the mid-1990s", Columbia University, New York City, 2015.

[CLA 99] CLARKE I., "A distributed decentralised information storage and retrieval system", unpublished report, *Division of Informatics*, University of Edinburgh, available at: http://www.freenet project.org, 1999.

[CLA 00] CLARKE I., SANDBERG O., WILEY B. *et al.*, "Freenet, a distributed anonymous information storage and retrieval system", *Lecture Notes in Computer Science*, Springer, Berlin/Heidelberg, 2000.

[DAR 09] DARDOT P., LAVAL C., *La nouvelle raison du monde. Essai sur la société néolibérale*, La Découverte, Paris, 2009.

[DEL 96] DELAHAYE J.-P., "Information noyée, information cachée", *Pour la science*, vol. 229, 1996.

[DEM 02] DEMBART L., "Give Big Brother the slip", *International Herald Tribune*, available at: http://www.uni-muenster.de/PeaCon/global-texte/g-w/n/peekabooty.htm, 2002.

[DIF 76] DIFFIE W., HELLMAN M., "New directions in cryptography", *IEEE Transactions on Information Theory*, vol. 22, no. 6, 1976.

[DI 14] DI LASCIO F., "Espace public et droit administratif", *Philonsorbonne*, no. 8, pp. 133–143, 2014.

[DUV 98] DUVAL G., "Internet: faut-il privatiser le réseau mondial?", *Alternatives économiques*, no. 158, available at: http://www.alternatives-economiques.fr/internet-faut-privatiser-reseau-mondial/00018736, 1998.

[GEL 13] GELLMAN B., TIMBERG C., RICH S., "Secret NSA documents show campaign against Tor encrypted network", *The Washington Post*, 2013.

[GOL 99] GOLDSCHAG D., REED M., SYVERSON P., "Onion routing for anonymous and private Internet connections", *Communications of the ACM*, vol. 42, 1999.

[GOM 16] GOMBERT D.C., CEVALLOS A.S., GARAFOLA C.L., *War with China. Thinking through the Unthinkable*, RAND Corporation, Santa Monica, California, available at: http://www.rand.org/pubs/research_reports/RR1140.html, 2016.

[GRE 00] GREENFELD K.T., "Meet the Napster", *Time*, available at: http://content.time.com/time/world/ article/0,8599,2053826,00.html, 2000.

[GUL 05] GULLI A., SIGNORINI A., "Building an open source meta-search engine", *14th International Conference on the World Wide Web*, China, Japan, May 10–14, 2005.

[HAB 93] HABERMAS J., *L'Espace public : Archéologie de la publicité comme dimension constitutive de la société bourgeoise*, Payot, Paris, 1993.

[HUG 93] HUGHES E., "Manifeste d'un Cypherpunk", available at: https://www. activisme.fr/cypherpunks/manifesto.html, 1993.

[JAR 15] JARDINE E., "The dark web dilemma: tor, anonymity and online policing", *Global Commission on Internet Governance, Paper series*, no. 21, available at: https://www.cigionline.org/ sites/default/files/no.21.pdf, 2015.

[JOH 07] JOHNSON E., MCGUIRE D., WILLEY N.D., "The security risk of peer-to-peer file sharing networks", Center for Digital Strategies, Tuck School of Business, 2007.

[JOH 13] JOHNSON A., WACEK C., JANSEN R. *et al.*, *US Naval Research Laboratory*, Georgetown University, Washington, DC ACM, 2013.

[KER 83] KERCKHOFFS A., "La cryptographie militaire", *Journal des sciences militaires*, vol. IX, pp. 5–38, 1883, 1883.

[LAW 14] LAWRENCE D., "The Inside Story of Tor, the Best Internet Anonymity Tool the Government ever Built", *Bloomberg Business Week*, available at: https://www.bloomberg.com/news/articles/2014-01-23/tor-anonymity-software-vs-dot-the-national-security-agency, 2014.

[LEW 91] LEWYN M., SCHWARTZ E.I., "Why 'The Legion of Doom' has little fear of the Feds", available at: www.bloomberg.com, 1991.

[LIE 07] LIEBAU N., PUSSEP K., GRAFFI K. *et al.*, "The impact of the P2P Paradigm on the new media industries", AMCIS 7, *Proceedings of Americas Conference on Information Systems*, 2007.

[LOV 16] LOVECRUFT I., cited in "Shari Steele on online anonymity: Tor's staff are freedom fighters", *The Guardian*, available at: https://www.theguardian.com/technology/2016/jan/11/shari-steele-tor-encryption-online-anonymity-censorship, 2016.

[MAD 15] MADDOX A., BARRATT M.J., ALLEN M. *et al.*, Constructive activism in the dark web: cryptomarkets and illicit drugs in the digital 'demimonde', *Information, Communication & Society*, pp. 1-29, 1–16, October 2015.

[MAY 94] MAY T.C., "Crypto anarchy and virtual communities", available at: http://groups.csail.mit.edu/mac/xclasses/6.805/articles/crypto/cypherpunks/may-virtual-comm.html, 1994.

[MOO 16] MOORE D., RID T., "Cryptopolitik and the Darknet", *Survival: Global Politics and Strategy, International Institute for Strategic Studies*, vol. 58, 2016.

[MUE 17] MUELLER M., *Will the Internet Fragment?*, Polity Press, 2017.

[MUR 00] MURRAY B.H., CYVEILLANCE, "Sizing the Internet", available at: http://www.cyveillance.com/ web/downloads/Sizing_the_Internet.pdf, 2000.

[NUN 16] NUNES E., DIAB A., GUNN A. *et al.*, *Darknet and Deepnet Mining for Proactive Cybersecurity Threat Intelligence*, Arizona State University, 2016.

[OMA 12] OMAND S.D., BARTLETT J., MILLER C., *Intelligence. Intelligence and National Security*, Demos, London, 2012.

[OMA 16] OMAND S.D., "The dark net: policing the Internet's underworld", World Policy Journal, 2016.

[PAQ 11] PAQUOT T., *L'Espace public*, Éditions La Découverte, 2011.

[PIS 08] PISANI F., PIOTET D., *Comment le web change le monde: l'alchimie des multitudes*, Pearson, 2008.

[POR 16] PORUP J.M., "Building a new Tor that can resist next-generation state surveillance", *Ars technical*, available at: https://arstechnica.com/security/2016/08/building-a-new-tor-that-withstands-next-generation-state-surveillance/, 2016.

[QIA 06] QIAO L., WANG X., *La guerre hors limites*, Rivages Poches, 2006.

[REI 99] REITER M.K., RUBIN A.D., "Anonymous web transactions with *Crowds*", *Communications of the ACM*, vol. 42, no. 2, 1999.

[REN 16] RENNARD J.-P., *Darknet: Mythes et réalités*, Ellipses, 2016.

[RID 11] RID T., "Cyber war will not take place", *Journal of Strategic Studies*, vol. 35, no. 1, 2011.

[RIV 78] RIVEST R.L., SHAMIR A., ADLEMAN L., "A method for obtaining digital signatures and public-key cryptosystems", *Communications of the ACM*, vol. 21, no. 2, 1978.

[ROB 15] ROBINSON T., "Shari Steele named executive director for the Tor Project", *SC Media*, available at: https://www.scmagazine.com/former-eff-executive-director-takes-reins-at-tor-project/article/533161/, 2015.

[SEN 79] SENNETT R., *Les tyrannies de l'intimité*, Le Seuil, Paris, 1979.

[STE 92] STERLING B., *The Hacker Crackdown: Law and Disorder on the Electronic Frontier*, Bantam Books, New York, 1992.

[STE 99] STERLING B., *Hackers: Crime in the Digital Sublime*, Routledge, 1999.

[STE 15] STEELE S., "New Tor director Shari Steele gears up for challenging future (Q&A)", *The Parallax*, available at: https://www.the-parallax.com/2015/12/30/new-tor-director-shari-steele-gears-up-for-challenging-future-qa/, 2015.

[STO 15] STOCKLEY M., "Onion.city – a search engine bringing the Dark Web into the light", *Naked Security*, available at: https://nakedsecurity.sophos.com/2015/02/18/onion-city-a-search-engine-bringing-the-dark-web-into-the-light/, 2015.

[SYV 14] SYVERSON P., REED M.G., GOLDSCHLAG D.M., "Private Web Browsing", Naval Research Laboratory, 2 June 1997, cited by LEVINE Y., "Almost Everyone Involved in Developing Tor was (or is) Funded by the US Government", *Pando*, available at: https://pando.com/2014/07/16/tor-spooks/, 2014.

[TAR 14] TARLE (DE) A., "La privatisation d'Internet", *Déchiffrage-Europe 1/Le JDD*, 2014.

[WAT 98] WATTS D.J., STROGATZ S.H., "Collective dynamics of 'small-world' networks", *Nature*, vol. 393, pp. 440–442, 1998.

[WEI 16] WEIMANN G., "Going dark: terrorism on the dark web", *Studies in Conflict & Terrorism*, vol. 39, no. 3, 2016.

[WU 03] WU T., "Network Neutrality, Broadband discrimination", *Journal of Telecommunications and High Technology Law*, vol. 2, p. 141, 2003.

Index

S, T

server, 4, 7, 16, 27, 71–74, 81,
  95, 97, 100, 105, 120, 124
SIGINT, 60, 61
Soulseek, 76, 77
surface web, 10, 11, 47, 132
TCP/IP, 26, 32, 52
TLD, 35

U, W

UKUSA, 63
USENET, 63
WHOIS, 34–36, 39, 43

Other titles from

in

Information Systems, Web and Pervasive Computing

2018

ARDUIN Pierre-Emmanuel
Insider Threats
(Advances in Information Systems Set – Volume 10)

FABRE Renaud, BENSOUSSAN Alain
The Digital Factory for Knowledge: Production and Validation of Scientific
Results

GAUDIN Thierry, LACROIX Dominique, MAUREL Marie-Christine, POMEROL
Jean-Charles
Life Sciences, Information Sciences

IAFRATE Fernando
Artificial Intelligence and Big Data: The Birth of a New Intelligence
(Advances in Information Systems Set – Volume 8)

MANDRAN Nadine
Traceable Human Experiment Design Research: Theoretical Model and
Practical Guide
(Advances in Information Systems Set – Volume 9)

2017

BOUHAÏ Nasreddine, SALEH Imad
Internet of Things: Evolutions and Innovations
(Digital Tools and Uses Set – Volume 4)

DUONG Véronique
Baidu SEO: Challenges and Intricacies of Marketing in China

LESAS Anne-Marie, MIRANDA Serge
The Art and Science of NFC Programming
(Intellectual Technologies Set – Volume 3)

LIEM André
Prospective Ergonomics
(Human-Machine Interaction Set – Volume 4)

MARSAULT Xavier
Eco-generative Design for Early Stages of Architecture
(Architecture and Computer Science Set – Volume 1)

REYES-GARCIA Everardo
The Image-Interface: Graphical Supports for Visual Information
(Digital Tools and Uses Set – Volume 3)

REYES-GARCIA Everardo, BOUHAÏ Nasreddine
Designing Interactive Hypermedia Systems
(Digital Tools and Uses Set – Volume 2)

SAÏD Karim, BAHRI KORBI Fadia
Asymmetric Alliances and Information Systems:Issues and Prospects
(Advances in Information Systems Set – Volume 7)

SZONIECKY Samuel, BOUHAÏ Nasreddine
Collective Intelligence and Digital Archives: Towards Knowledge
Ecosystems
(Digital Tools and Uses Set – Volume 1)

2016

BEN CHOUIKHA Mona
Organizational Design for Knowledge Management

BERTOLO David
Interactions on Digital Tablets in the Context of 3D Geometry Learning
(Human-Machine Interaction Set – Volume 2)

BOUVARD Patricia, SUZANNE Hervé
Collective Intelligence Development in Business

EL FALLAH SEGHROUCHNI Amal, ISHIKAWA Fuyuki, HÉRAULT Laurent,
TOKUDA Hideyuki
Enablers for Smart Cities

FABRE Renaud, in collaboration with MESSERSCHMIDT-MARIET Quentin,
HOLVOET Margot
New Challenges for Knowledge

GAUDIELLO Ilaria, ZIBETTI Elisabetta
Learning Robotics, with Robotics, by Robotics
(Human-Machine Interaction Set – Volume 3)

HENROTIN Joseph
The Art of War in the Network Age
(Intellectual Technologies Set – Volume 1)

KITAJIMA Munéo
Memory and Action Selection in Human–Machine Interaction
(Human–Machine Interaction Set – Volume 1)

LAGRAÑA Fernando
E-mail and Behavioral Changes: Uses and Misuses of Electronic
Communications

LEIGNEL Jean-Louis, UNGARO Thierry, STAAR Adrien
Digital Transformation
(Advances in Information Systems Set – Volume 6)

NOYER Jean-Max
Transformation of Collective Intelligences
(Intellectual Technologies Set – Volume 2)

VENTRE Daniel
Information Warfare – 2ⁿᵈ edition

VITALIS André
The Uncertain Digital Revolution
(Computing and Connected Society Set – Volume 1)

2015

ARDUIN Pierre-Emmanuel, GRUNDSTEIN Michel, ROSENTHAL-SABROUX Camille
Information and Knowledge System
(Advances in Information Systems Set – Volume 2)

BÉRANGER Jérôme
Medical Information Systems Ethics

BRONNER Gérald
Belief and Misbelief Asymmetry on the Internet

IAFRATE Fernando
From Big Data to Smart Data
(Advances in Information Systems Set – Volume 1)

KRICHEN Saoussen, BEN JOUIDA Sihem
Supply Chain Management and its Applications in Computer Science

NEGRE Elsa
Information and Recommender Systems
(Advances in Information Systems Set – Volume 4)

POMEROL Jean-Charles, EPELBOIN Yves, THOURY Claire
MOOCs

2012

BUCHER Bénédicte, LE BER Florence
Innovative Software Development in GIS

GAUSSIER Eric, YVON François
Textual Information Access

STOCKINGER Peter
Audiovisual Archives: Digital Text and Discourse Analysis

VENTRE Daniel
Cyber Conflict

2011

BANOS Arnaud, THÉVENIN Thomas
Geographical Information and Urban Transport Systems

DAUPHINÉ André
Fractal Geography

LEMBERGER Pirmin, MOREL Mederic
Managing Complexity of Information Systems

STOCKINGER Peter
Introduction to Audiovisual Archives

STOCKINGER Peter
Digital Audiovisual Archives

VENTRE Daniel
Cyberwar and Information Warfare

2010

BONNET Pierre
Enterprise Data Governance

BRUNET Roger
Sustainable Geography

GUERMOND Yves
Modeling Process in Geography

KANEVSKI Michael
Advanced Mapping of Environmental Data

MANOUVRIER Bernard, LAURENT Ménard
Application Integration: EAI, B2B, BPM and SOA

PAPY Fabrice
Digital Libraries

2007

DOBESCH Hartwig, DUMOLARD Pierre, DYRAS Izabela
Spatial Interpolation for Climate Data

SANDERS Lena
Models in Spatial Analysis

2006

CLIQUET Gérard
Geomarketing

CORNIOU Jean-Pierre
Looking Back and Going Forward in IT

DEVILLERS Rodolphe, JEANSOULIN Robert
Fundamentals of Spatial Data Quality

Printed and bound by CPI Group (UK) Ltd, Croydon, CR0 4YY